White House in a Gray City

Written and Illustrated
by Itzchak Belfer

A Child of
Janusz Korczak

Books that Love Children

In memory of my parents, brothers, sisters, grandmother, and grandfather, whose place of murder remains unknown.

In memory of Janusz Korczak, Stefa Wilczynska, and the children murdered by the Nazis.

I dedicate this book to them.

White House in a Gray City / Itzchak Belfer

Translated into English: Ora Baumgarten
Drawing and Sculptures: Itzchak Belfer
Production: Haim Belfer

Website: www.itzchakbelfer.com
Contact: itzchakbelfer@gmail.com

ISBN 978-1981480067

White House
in a **Gray City**

Itzchak Belfer

A Child of Janusz Korczak

Contents

ACKNOWLEDGEMENTS

My numerous acquaintances have often urged me to commit my memories to writing. It was painful for me to undertake the recollection of those distant days of suffering and fear, and to reencounter family members whom I loved so dearly and who are no longer with us.

Janusz Korczak and Stefa Wilczynska represent a ray of light and beacon along the somber journey of my life, from childhood in the orphanage under their direction, to this very day. Thanks to them, I have adopted a way of life based on values of humanity, honesty, justice, and consideration for others. Thanks to their theories and pedagogy, I have managed to overcome obstacles and to create a positive dialogue with people and the world in which I live.

It was my fortune to have met Varda Segal, whose profound artistic talents as a designer and documenter were already known to me in the past. Varda agreed to undertake this task with me and the rapport between the two of us led to a common language, the product of which is this book. I wish to express my deepest appreciation and thanks to Varda for the patience and personal involvement she demonstrated in our discussions and meetings.

I warmly thank my dear ones, my wife Shoshi, and my son Haim, without whose support and assistance this book would never have been published.

FOREWORD

I was born into a tragic and stormy period, between the First and Second World Wars. Those were days of hope followed by nights of disillusionment. I struggled and groped to survive and to keep afloat in the world. The events of this period have been woven into the very fabric of my life.

I was brought up with a strong Jewish awareness in an Orthodox home with my mother, father, and grandparents in Warsaw of the 1920s. I was but a child when my father died. After my father's death, I was accepted into Dr. Korczak's home for orphans.

The orphanage was founded on democratic and egalitarian educational values that characterized Dr. Korczak's theories. Life at the orphanage opened a whole new horizon for me, affecting my entire world view. Those two dear people, Dr. Korczak and his associate, the admired educator, Miss Stefa Wilczynska, left their mark on me and, to a large extent, molded my personality. I have adhered to their doctrines throughout the course of my life.

The Second World War unsettled the world order, turning

my own life upside down. Never again was I to be a young boy sipping life's pleasures, living through new experiences, and making my way toward adulthood. I matured against my will and became a master of my own fate. My sole purpose was to claim responsibility for my own survival.

During the Second World War, the free world was defeated by evil forces of the Nazi regime. Those dark and painful days left a deep scar upon the spirit of my people, the Jewish people.

I have visions of the Holocaust, of the Warsaw Ghetto, before and after the war. Never again will my eyes behold the images of my loved ones. I can still hear the horrific accounts of the Holocaust sounding in my ears to this day, just as I did when I first heard them. I do not forget anything. My thoughts often take me back to that time.

Working as a sketch artist and sculptor, I have, over the course of my life, endeavored to express my pain, grief, and loss. I totally identify with the suffering of others. I hope and believe that sanity will eventually return to our lives.

At a certain point in my life, I resolved to direct my art toward the stories of those who did not survive the Holocaust, and toward the commemoration of those responsible for my happy childhood experiences.

I am often overwhelmed by the feeling that however hard I try, my story will never succeed in doing justice to the huge contribution of Janusz Korczak and Miss Stefa made to the Jewish people and to the field of education. These two dear people provided me with my "toolbox for life," which I cherish to this day. I have felt an obligation to learn, explore, digest, and disseminate their unique educational enterprise. Dr.

Korczak and Miss Stefa remained close to my heart during the darkest of times and throughout my entire life. Both exist within the pages of this book, narrating my personal story.

This book is a memorial volume.

"I lived in close proximity to him for ten years.

"I have lived my entire life in his light."

Itzchak Belfer

INTRODUCTION:
Events of the Period

D r. Henryk Goldschmidt was known by his pen name, Janusz Korczak. He was an author, intellectual, and pioneering pedagogue who developed an educational theory that has left its mark on the educational world.

He was also a pediatrician, who abandoned an outstanding medical practice to become the director of a Jewish orphanage. The orphanage was the initiative of the Aid for Orphans organization of the Jewish community in Warsaw, Poland.

At the outbreak of the First World War in 1914, Dr. Korczak was recruited as a military doctor. In his absence, Miss Stefa took over the management of the orphanage in the spirit of Dr. Korczak's educational principles, with the cooperation of the children themselves.

At the end of the war four years later, on his return to the orphanage, the doctor was warmly welcomed by the entire "family"—the children and the staff of the orphanage. Dr. Korczak's pedagogical credo, entitled *How to Love a Child,* was published at that time. His subsequent book, *The Child's Right to Respect*, was published ten years later.

Dr. Korczak contracted typhus during his military service. The disease worsened in 1919, obliging him to retire to his mother's home for convalescence. While Dr. Korczak's physical condition improved, his mother also contracted typhus and passed away thereafter. Dr. Korczak returned to the orphanage depressed and guilt-stricken and wrote his essay entitled "The Educator's Prayer," which he dedicated to his mother and father.

The orphanage was managed as a family unit. The "father" was occupied with his own affairs and was frequently away from home, while the "mother" figure bore the burden of taking care of the home and the upbringing of the children.

Stefania Wilczynska, generally known as "Miss Stefa," was the matron of the orphanage and she managed the institution during the war. Miss Stefa, with her outstanding personality and excellent organizational skills, meticulously implemented Dr. Korczak's educational theories. As far as their characters were concerned, Dr. Korczak and Stefa complemented each other, together forming a team that conducted its mission through understanding, trust, mutual respect, and consideration of the children's special needs. Both worked voluntarily.

Miss Stefa's beautiful, kind eyes missed nothing. She often wore a black gown with a white collar. Her footsteps made no sound as she floated swiftly through the rooms of the orphanage in her black shoes. She would compliment a child, pat another child, reprimand someone else, and then immediately extend a loving hug of reconciliation.

Dr. Henryk Goldschmidt—Janusz Korczak

Miss Stefania (Stefa) Wilczynska

In addition to her work at the orphanage, Miss Stefa cultivated close ties with *Eretz Israel,* the Land of Israel, or Palestine as it was then called, especially with her friend Feiga Lipschitz of Kibbutz Ein Harod. Previously an educator at the orphanage, Feiga hosted Miss Stefa during her three visits to Israel. Dr. Korczak, too, visited Kibbutz Ein Harod twice, following Stefa's fervent support of Jewish settlement in general and kibbutz life in particular. He returned to Warsaw from these visits in a state of elation.

At the end of his first visit, the doctor wrote in his diary: "Witnessing the efforts to revive the Land of Israel, the language, the people, their fate and beliefs, beholding the coast of Haifa in the distance, caused me to believe that the prayer expressed once a year on the festival of Passover, 'Next year in Jerusalem,' has indeed been granted. This is the edge of the Diaspora. I have been given the right to return to the Land of Israel after 2,000 years of wandering and persecution."

Both the doctor and Miss Stefa came to the conclusion that their rightful home was the Land of Israel, to which they were both drawn by a seemingly magical and invisible cord. Believing that their contribution toward the development of the orphanage was complete, they resigned from its management in 1937. Surprisingly enough, the children had no inkling of their resignation, and we felt their presence as usual throughout that period. For our part, our home continued to function as it always had.

Dr. Korczak moved to his sister's home, while Miss Stefa, who had applied to the British authorities in Palestine for an immigration permit (*sertifikat*), worked as a national inspector at CENTOS, a Jewish organization for orphanage institutions. In 1938, Miss Stefa received her long-awaited permit and immigrated to Israel, settling on Kibbutz Ein Harod and working in the children's home.

Unfortunately, Dr. Korczak was obliged to remain in Warsaw owing to prior commitments and he worked untiringly on arrangements for his own immigration. However, Miss Stefa caught wind of the ominous stirrings in Europe, packed her meager belongings, and returned to Warsaw to assist her colleague. Ultimately, neither of them succeeded in fulfilling their dream of *aliyah*.

Dr. Korczak and Miss Stefa resumed the management of the orphanage at the outbreak of the Second World War. Warsaw surrendered to the Germans after collapsing under German bombs and shells. At the time, both Dr. Korczak and Stefa were busy extinguishing fires that resulted from the bombing on the rooftop of the orphanage to which they had returned, and figurative fires that inevitably erupted through the reality of survival.

Dr. Korczak feverishly sought sources of economic assistance, food, and supplies while Miss Stefa organized a first aid station in one of the rooms of the orphanage. She extended medical assistance to residents of the orphanage and to the people around that area. All of this activity was carried out through a discussion of the question: "Should the orphanage remain open, or should it close down and all the children be returned to their homes and their destinies?" The doctor decided to take responsibility for the children's lives and took even more children under his wing. The number of young children in the home rose to 150.

1940

The Nazis forced the Jews of Warsaw to wear Star of David bands and to live within the limits of the Warsaw Ghetto. The orphanage staff, together with the children, left the home on 92 Krochmalna Street with only a small portion of their possessions.

During the move, the Germans confiscated a cart carrying potatoes, which the doctor had procured with great difficulty for the children. The furious Dr. Korczak reported this matter to the Gestapo offices, demanding the return of his cart. The question of his Jewish origins was raised during the ensuing discussion. "In that case," he was reprimanded, "why are you not wearing the Star of David identification band?" He was sent to prison but the cart of potatoes was returned to the orphanage.

While Dr. Korczak was in prison, Miss Stefa was left on her own to bear responsibility for the management of the orphanage and organize the move in a totally unsuitable and inadequate building, while seeking resources for their survival. After three months of imprisonment, three of Dr. Korczak's former orphanage children paid the Germans a heavy ransom, following which the Germans discharged Dr. Korczak from prison. He returned to his duties at the orphanage, which by then already held 200 children.

Overcrowding, poverty, hunger, poor hygienic conditions, disease, and lack of medical supplies were becoming apparent. The mortality rate of the Jews in the ghetto began to rise and Dr. Korczak spent night and day attempting to find food and medication for his children. He would ignore the curfews and leave the ghetto, thereby endangering his own life.

Miss Stefa and the orphanage staff carried on the management of the home according to Dr. Korczak's principles. That Passover, donors were invited to participate in the *Seder*[1] in appreciation of their contribution to the home.

At the beginning of the Jewish New Year, tickets were sold for the Jewish New Year, *Yom Kippur*,[2] and *Sukkot*[3] worship services. The main hall of the home was converted into a synagogue, proudly containing a Torah ark with two Torah scrolls inside. A cantor sang the litanies with fervent meaning, directing the prayers to the Almighty in heaven.

The doctor could be seen in one of the corners of the hall, engrossed in a *Rosh Hashanah*[4] prayer book, translated into Polish.

---

1   Jewish ritual feast that marks the beginning of the Jewish holiday of Passover.

2   Day of Atonement

3   Feast of Tabernacles

4   Jewish New Year

In search of food

1941

The Germans decide
to reduce the size of the ghetto

In 1941, the orphanage was obliged to move into yet another building, much smaller and more crowded than the previous one. Miss Stefa, with her typical efficiency and organizational skills, performed the impossible task of creating a home for the children in the new space. The orphanage lacked food and heating, and the cold winter froze its inhabitants to the bone.

In 1942, Dr. Korczak became aware of the desperate situation and high mortality rate in the Central Organization for the Care of Orphans and Abandoned Children in the ghetto. He subsequently took a month off from the management of the orphanage and assumed responsibility for managing the center, to assist in rehabilitating and improving conditions there.

Dr. Korczak expressed his grief: "I have decided to confine myself to the infamous concentration camp in the Jewish quarter. If one can believe the public outcry, it is said that tens of children die in the ghetto daily. This is indeed an act of suicide, but I must try to do my best."

He indeed made an attempt to rescue as many children as possible and succeeded to an unbelievable extent. At the end of that month, the mortality rate decreased and almost ceased completely. Faithful to his decision, even after his return to his own home, Dr. Korczak continued to visit the orphanage where he offered advice and assistance to the children.

Dr. Korczak wrote in his diary: "Oh God in Heaven, this prayer which I offer you was created through hunger and misfortune."

Approximately a month and a half before the final deportation of its inhabitants, the orphanage staged a play, which was banned by the Nazis. The play, based on a legend written by the Indian author, Rabindranath Tagore, was initiated by the doctor, who believed in providing emotional support through optimism.

The invitations to the production read, "We have no intention of promising anything of which we are unsure. We believe that an hour of watching a legend written by a philosopher and poet will provide hope, the highest rung on the emotional ladder. We therefore invite you to attend on Saturday, 7/18/1942, at four-thirty in the afternoon." Signed: The Director of the Orphanage, Goldschmidt-Korczak.

Wednesday,
8.5.1942

"All Jews Out"

The hobnail boots of the Nazi oppressors entered the orphanage with a chilling sound of commands being shouted. In contrast to the situation, Stefa composedly dressed the frightened children in clothes she had prepared ahead of time, supporting the children and calming them down. The small children obediently gathered outside in the orphanage courtyard where the doctor and his staff arranged them in four columns.

The death march had begun. The first stop was the collection point, the *Umschlagplatz*.

The column of people moved through the alleyways of the ghetto and streets of Warsaw. There were more than 200 souls, their hearts pounding with fear. Dr. Korczak led the ranks. Next were the children, from the smallest to the tallest. Miss Stefa and the staff of teachers marched in the middle and the administration staff were at the end of the line. Both sides of the column were flanked by fully uniformed German soldiers holding loaded rifles, in contrast to the people marching between them.

The silence of the street seemed deafening. The street was packed with Polish residents of Warsaw, watching the gaunt, withered figures, bearing the marks of two years of suffering in the Warsaw Ghetto, walking in procession, with white bands bearing light blue Stars of David. These were Jews, supporting each other and infusing their stumbling friends with the little strength they had left.

"We will soon be there," the doctor encouraged his children. "Just a little more and then we will rest. A train will take us from the collection point to another place. A better one," the compassionate doctor whispered with his remaining strength.

There is no record of their arrival at Treblinka, the Nazi extermination camp, situated about one hundred miles from Warsaw.

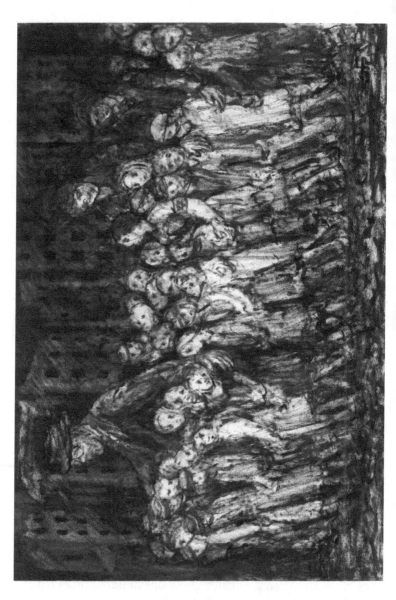

On their final journey

Mother

CHAPTER 1:

215 Wolska Street, Warsaw

"I do not exist in order to be loved or cherished, but rather to act and to love."

"I do not expect my surroundings to be of assistance to me, rather I must care about the entire world and about people around me."

- Janusz Korczak.

A small building with a slanted roof stands at the end of Wolska Street, number 215. This two-story house looks modest; its walls are made of wooden slats and its windows are cut into the walls, lying wide open to the street. This is the house of my childhood.

My grandparents resided on the first floor of the building in an apartment containing two rooms and a kitchen. The six rooms on the second floor housed six families, each blessed with many children. One of those families was mine. There were seven people in the family—my mother, my brothers and sisters, and me. Every corner of the apartment was filled with signs of life, overcrowding, and poverty.

The basement of the building contained a room for storing coal used for our heating, various unused items, and vegetables such as potatoes, beets, and cabbages. A church was a stone's throw from the house. The residents of the street were both Christians and Jews, all coexisting in peace.

My name is Itzchak—known as Itzchakeleh in my childhood. I was the fourth child to my parents, Esther Bernstein and Haim Belfer. My oldest brother, Moshe, was about ten when I was born, Alter was about seven, my sister Chaya was about three, Velvaleh (Wolf) was born two years after me, and the youngest child was Miriam, who sprang into the world when I was four years old. I was born on 2.6.1923.

When my father died, we moved into my grandparents' house. I was about four years old. I have vague and distant memories of another house, beautiful and spacious, the house where my mother, father, and siblings had previously lived until pneumonia took my father from us. My mother was approaching the end of her pregnancy and remained a widow while we became fatherless. My youngest sister, Miriam, was born after my father's death.

I have very few vague memories of my early years of childhood. I was told that my father had been a painter, repairman, and tradesman. I can barely conjure up an image of him. However, a hazy memory has sprung to mind:

My father and I are sitting on a *bryczka*[5] drawn by a white horse with brown spots, a horse I loved dearly. We were on our way out of Warsaw to buy fruit from an orchard. The unripe fruit was bought for purposes of trade.

I clearly remember my mother's large, black eyes. These kind eyes looked at us, her children, and at others around her with concern, tenderness, and sadness. Despite the over-crowded conditions, my widowed mother created a warm and pleasant nest for us in my grandparents' home. Besides taking care of her children and all the routine concerns of the house-hold, my mother laundered, cleaned, cooked, and found the time and stamina to mend and patch other people's clothing to earn a few extra pennies for our upkeep.

I did not have daily contact with my two older brothers. Having left their childhood behind them, they set out each morning to work to help with the upkeep of the family.

I had limited contact with my sister Chaya. She was already a young lady, also already working. I sometimes used to converse with her or visit her at her place of work. She would always give me a hug and some pocket money from her meager wages to buy a candy or a treat.

I have a distinct memory of my grandfather, Yehezkel, my mother's father who took us into his home. I see his face staring at me over the years. I try to conjure up his image, to cement it into my works of art. I mainly remember a long, white beard. He wore a large, black skullcap on his gray hair. His clothes were black, his body strong, and he walked

---

5   Small horse-drawn cart with two wheels.

proudly. On Sabbath days and festivals he would take my small hand in his warm one and we would walk together to prayers. As the *gabai*[6] of our local synagogue, he would take his seat on the pulpit reserved for distinguished persons. I would sit at his feet.

Grandfather made his living as a horse and cart owner. The cart drivers were hired Polish men. The stables were in the backyard and the carts were in front of the building. Every morning, the horses were harnessed and the cart drivers went out to work, loading bricks from the nearby factory and unloading them at various sites.

After watering and washing the horses at the nearby lake on Friday afternoons, the cart drivers would come to our home to collect their wages. Grandfather would give them a glass of Sabbath wine and a piece of *challah*[7] torn off by hand. Together they would bless the *Shabbat HaMalka*,[8] the religious Jew with the Polish gentiles.

Ours was a traditional Jewish home. I remember my grandmother, Henia, after finishing her housework, sitting down with the *Gemara*[9] open on the table, concentrating on her Talmud. She was so engrossed that she would not allow anything to interrupt her study of the Torah. If I approached her at those times, trying to get her attention, she would

---

6   Manager of synagogue affairs.

7   Traditional bread eaten by Jews.

8   The Sabbath Queen

9   Part of the Talmud that contains commentary on the Mishnah, part of the Oral Law of the Jewish religion.

dismiss me with a candy that she swept out of her dress and the wave of her hand, which meant "Away with you!" And where could I go?

The house was crowded. There was not enough room in the living room since the beds, which we shared, took up most of the space. Mother slept on the shelf of the fireplace that heated up the chilly winters. There were other pieces of furniture, which left hardly any place for recreation. The children's toys were always getting in the way of the adults in the house.

Outside, the harsh winter covered Warsaw and Poland with a freezing white blanket of snow. Most people remained in their houses, trying to stay warm by the crackling flames of the fireplace. The few people outside were rushing about, wrapped up in their heavy coats, hats, and gloves, bundled up to keep out the lashing wind.

The children did not play much outside except for the times when we gathered together to build snowmen, have snowball fights, or skate, shrieking with delight.

Then suddenly, out of nowhere, a rainbow appeared and a burst of joyful spring began to melt the frost, warming our hearts, enchanting us all with colorful blossoms, and the intoxicating smells of nature reinventing itself all around us. We swooped down on the verdant fields, gulping down the pleasure of open space.

The summers shuffling in after the spring were short and hot. Thunder and lightning storms brought down furious rains, creating puddles on the warm ground. How I loved to jump barefoot into the warm puddles, play around, and run wild, splashing water all over the place.

There was a little bridge leading to our house, crossing over a canal. Water flowed from the melting snows to the lake beside the fields around our neighborhood. When the flow stopped, the parched canal became my playground. Crawling under that bridge was my favorite pastime, my imagination leading me to pleasurable places.

After the summer, the fall dragged its dismal trail. The winds once again started blowing and the sky filled with heavy clouds. Spurts of rain washed the world around our house. My nose was pressed against the window pane, and I dismally watched the world outside, sad and bored until the end of the winter.

Again it was winter and the white snow erased the spring colors. As usual, the sun sought refuge from the cold behind the clouds.

Warsaw of those days embodied a huge center of Orthodox Jewry. Warsaw Jews created a flourishing and impressive culture whose impact on all of Polish Jewry was significant.

Some of Warsaw's Jewish intellectuals were affiliated with the general Polish population. In addition, there were many Jewish institutions interspersed over the city, such as *Beit Ha-va'ad*,[10] synagogues, schools, *yeshivot*,[11] clinics, and a hospital. Jews spoke mostly Yiddish. There was also a *Talmud Torah*[12] school from which I was not exempt.

---

10   Meeting place

11   Rabbinical colleges

12   Parochial elementary school for boys.

I made my way every morning to the *cheder*[13] near the synagogue. Candles illuminated the winter darkness. At sunrise, rays of light capered gaily through the window. There I sat for hours on end with the other children, bored, falling asleep, and then waking up to the rising voice of the teacher repeating the *alef beis*[14] or the sound of the rabbi's *kancik*[15] which reduced one of my classmates to tears of pain.

Another image of my childhood was the topic of water. There was a hut not far from our house, toward the center of town. A faucet was attached to one of the side walls of the hut. When we required water, we would fill a bucket or two from that faucet, paying a woman for the water through a window in the wall. If we could not for some reason carry the water by ourselves, the old bent-backed water bearer would do so for several pennies. He had shoulder poles and the buckets would rock from side to side. Years later, I sketched that water bearer.

How can I conclude the story of the Jewish home without mentioning the *hamin?*[16] This was, after all, the best part, the climax of the Jewish Sabbath.

It all started on Fridays at noon. A procession of women, men, and children carrying pots marched down the street. Their destination was the bakery. The pots that were placed in

---

13   A school for Jewish children in which Hebrew and religious knowledge is taught.

14   Alphabet

15   Cane

16   Also known as cholent—a traditional Jewish stew.

the baker's oven would be retrieved after the *Shacharit*[17] and *Mussaf*[18] prayers. The procession made its way back home, the smell of the dish permeating the air.

As a young boy, mother occasionally sent me to the bakery carrying the pot of *hamin* and on Saturdays, my sister Chaya joined me. I carried our pot while she carried that of my grandparents.

Without the aid of my grandparents, Yehezkel and Henia, my family's survival would have been unbearably difficult. It was they who opened their home to us and supported us financially when my father passed away.

---

17   Daily morning prayer

18   Additional service that is recited on Sabbath and holidays.

CHAPTER 2:

A White House in a Gray City

(The Orphanage of Dr. Janusz Korczak, Warsaw, 92 Krochmalna Street)

"Children and youth make up one-third of the human race and they are entitled to one-third of humanity's resources."

- Janusz Korczak

My mother and I stood before an iron gate supported by a high walled fence. I was almost seven years old. My small hand gripped hers. I suppose she said something to the effect of, "That's it, my child, we are here." The gate opened, exposing a huge courtyard in which several children were playing. This courtyard represented an entirely new world for me.

A large, impressive building stood at the far side of the

courtyard, exactly how I had imagined it. The Jewish orphanage of Dr. Korczak was a four-story house with many windows on 92 Krochmalna Street. On one side of the building, there was a factory and on the other side were workers' houses. The neighborhood was predominantly Christian, a point that I shall discuss at a later stage.

When my mother became widowed, she was burdened with our upkeep. Possibly urged by my grandparents and others, she decided to move me into the orphanage that had an excellent reputation. Why did she choose me specifically? First of all, popular demand resulted in the orphanage policy, which was to accept only one child from each family. Secondly, I happened to be seven years old, which was the age at which the orphanage accepted children. I was also small and thin, and perhaps they thought that I would receive suitable nutrition, good medical attention by Dr. Korczak, and of course, a proper education.

On that morning, my mother bathed me, brushed my hair, dressed me in my best clothes, held my hand, and said, "Come, Itzchakeleh, we are going to a new home today." I do not remember whether she told me that I was going to stay there permanently. I doubt whether I understood the implications of her words. I walked with her, crossing the courtyard toward the front door of the building, which also opened. We ascended several stairs and reached a beautiful and spacious hall.

A man led us cheerfully to a small room at the side of the hall. He sported a small beard that was blond and streaked with reddish patches. His kind eyes were pale blue behind a pair of glasses. I later learned that the small room, containing a table and two chairs, was called the "store." The man beckoned my mother to sit down, sat down himself and, as though it was the most natural thing to do, lifted me and sat me on his lap.

At first I felt uncomfortable about the close proximity to a stranger, but my discomfort gradually vanished as I felt the soothing effect of the man's warm embrace, while he and my mother engaged themselves in conversation.

I began to play with the man's beard that aroused my curiosity, wondering whether it was real and how it grew in that way. The man displayed no indication that I was perhaps bothering him. I started to feel a pleasant sense of security.

I then made another step. I put out my arms and embraced the man, holding on to him, and supporting my sitting position. I gained courage from the man's patient attitude and from my own curiosity, which to this day is one of my qualities. I raised myself slightly, rested my cheek against his, and inspected my surroundings through his eyeglasses. The man remained indifferent to my movements.

When the adults' conversation came to an end and my mother was about to leave, she said goodbye and gave me a kiss, saying, "I am going home, Itzchakeleh. You are staying here."

And there I stayed with him, the man who took my hand in his warm one. I felt comfortable and did not feel the need to cry. Still holding his hand, I was introduced to Yossi, my guardian, or *apotropos*. He was an older child whose role was to guide me through the ways of the orphanage, its rules, and regulations. "You can ask him any question you have," the man said. "He is responsible for your actions. You have no responsibility, but you must try to behave according to the rules."

The three of us then descended to the washroom. My hair was shaved and then I was bathed and dressed in new clothes. I was now clean, sweet smelling and relaxed. The man stroked my face gently with his kind hand, not sparing a pat for the guardian, and then went on his way.

This man was no other than Dr. Janusz Korczak, or Mr. Doctor, as we called him, who had given me such an embracing reception and had made the first few hours of my stay at the orphanage pleasant.

I gradually started to feel comfortable in this place that was beginning to feel like my new home.

My guardian first took me around the building to acclimatize me to my new surroundings. We looked inside all of the rooms and halls, and I received an explanation about each of them and the codes of behavior for each room. I could not absorb everything at once, being quite overwhelmed with the day's events, emotion, and fatigue.

It became evening and then night, and time for bed. There were two sleeping halls at the top floor of the orphanage. One was for boys, with fifty-one beds. Opposite it was the girls' hall, containing fifty-six beds.

"This is your bed. This is where you will sleep. Do not be afraid. A light will keep away the dark. A teacher will sleep with us. He will take care of us, guard us, approach us and comfort us if we need him," Yossi said calmingly.

My eyes opened wide in amazement. An entire bed to

myself! A clean, white sheet, spread out, stretched out over the bed and probably a pillow and blanket on top of it. The children's beds were close to each other, separated by a tin board, high on one side and low on the other. The closeness created a feeling of security and offered an opportunity for contact and familiarity.

If I desired the company of other children, I turned my face to the low side of the board to make eye contact with my neighbors. We chatted, laughed, told each other stories, and revealed our fears. If, however, I was very tired, I would turn to the other side, the high side of the board providing me with privacy and a signal to the other children to leave me to sleep. At any rate, lights were out at nine o'clock and. a night light was left on overnight. One of the youth leaders of the home would be on duty and stay with us, giving us a feeling of security. If a child cried, there was always someone who would approach him or her. If a child was ill, he or she would be soothed with a kind word or a pat.

The children in the neighboring beds told me endless stories about the orphanage. One would provide a kind or comforting word. Even the older children, whose beds were separate from each other, granted me a feeling of safety. Their stories were my proof that this was a good and worthy place in which to be.

Over the next few nights, I was introduced to the regular routine that slowly helped us sail into the world of sleep and dreams. This sometimes took the form of calming music that filled the sleeping halls, or else it was Mr. Doctor telling us a goodnight story, walking between the beds, patting a child there, fixing another's blanket there. If the doctor was absent or occupied in his work, one of the youth leaders would replace him. We were always allowed to read until lights out.

A new day dawns

I woke up to a new day at six in the morning. The air was fresh and filled the sleeping hall through the wide open windows. On cold winter days, I actually had the inclination to curl up and hide inside my blanket instead of getting out of bed. We overcame this temptation not only through our own self-discipline, but thanks to the tenderness, softness, kind words, and strokes that we received from the person who was on duty to wake up the children. He would move from child to child, coaxing and persuading him or her to get out of bed.

We eventually got up, made our beds, arranged the sheets, and folded the blankets. Then we washed ourselves, got dressed, and went down to the dining room. We were surprised to see Dr. Korczak standing on a small landing below the sleeping halls, at the side of which was a little room.

"Come, Itzchakeleh," he said, and showed me a note. "You see, here it says that everyone has to take cod-liver oil, and we are going to take it now. This oil is excellent for your health, and thanks to it, you will grow up healthy and strong." We reluctantly followed him since we knew we had to obey any instructions the doctor gave us.

On the landing, there was a table with little cups laid out.

In each of the cups was a thick, shiny, oily liquid. This was cod-liver oil. There was a little bowl with little pieces of bread beside the cups, next to which was another bowl containing salt.

"Come, my child," he said. "I will show you how to take this medicine. Do as I do and you will see how easy it is." Dr. Korczak took a piece of bread and so did I. He dipped his into the salt and I did the same. He held the bread in his hand and so did I. "Now, block your nose," he said, demonstrating on his own nose. I blocked my nose. "Now, take a glass and drink it all at once." I drank. Yuk! "And now, please eat the bread and see how tasty it is." It was really tasty! Being young and thin, I started the day with a glass of cod-liver oil for many months to come.

The weighing and measuring ceremony was held every Saturday morning. In turn, each child entered the small room where we were weighed and measured. All our details were registered on our personal growth charts, which accompanied us throughout our stay at the orphanage. One of Dr. Korczak's intentions was to write a book about the physical development of the child. The terrible war ahead was to destroy his wishes and hopes.

On the first morning of my stay at the orphanage, and for the following four months, I was accompanied by my guardian who provided me with explanations and instructed me in the workings of the orphanage. Together we entered the dining room, where the children were sitting down for breakfast at long tables. Everyone sat together—older children with

younger ones, teachers with children, girls with boys, Dr. Korczak and Miss Stefa among them. There was no distinction, division, or class system. Eight people sat at each table, all as equals.

Each person had a permanent seat at the table in the dining room for all the meals. If a child wished to switch places to sit next to a friend, he or she could negotiate the swap with the child with whom they wished to exchange seats. If that child agreed, the switch was made. Dr. Korczak and the teachers rarely interfered. The children managed their world by themselves. I shall discuss this aspect of our education later.

I was seated at a table. I must admit that my first breakfast at the orphanage was very pleasing to the palate. All of the meals at the orphanage took the same form. Today, as an adult, I understand that the aim was to educate us in rules, table manners, consideration of others, and sound eating habits.

The dining room bell sounded regularly three times a day inside the building and in the courtyard. Miss Stefa was usually in charge of ringing the bell. When we heard the bell, we all stopped whatever we were doing, went to wash our hands, and entered the dining room to take our regular places at the tables quietly, calmly and politely, without pushing, racing, or shouting.

The tables had already been set for the meal by the dining room helpers, who were children, chosen by the children themselves. The dining room duty roster was arranged once every few months, the children deciding upon the composition of each team. The dining room had the largest team of helpers.

There were two helpers in the kitchen, which was on the bottom floor of the building. An additional two helpers operated the small manual elevator that delivered the food from the kitchen to the dining room. This was no easy task; it required much responsibility and physical ability. If the helpers ran out of strength and lost their grip on the rope, the elevator would slip from their hands and fall all the way down, making a clamor while all the food splashed around it. Once the meal successfully made its way up to its destination, the two helpers in charge of the task would transfer the food and lay it out on the sideboard. Additional helpers served the plates and food to the tables. Yet another team was in charge of clearing the tables. And of course, at the end of the entire process, another team was in charge of piling up all the dishes for washing in the kitchen. Once again, the small elevator was loaded, this time for the return trip down to the kitchen.

A child was in charge of all the helping teams. It was his or her responsibility to make sure that everything ran smoothly. For example, he or she had to make sure that the children walked in from right to left, to and from each of the serving points and tables, so as to avoid collisions. The person in charge was the one who had the authority to approve or decline a request to switch duties or tasks.

To this day, I still remember the tranquility, contentment, and grace of those meals at the orphanage.

Miss Stefa attends to everything

We would go to the "store" for our supplies after breakfast. This was a small room at the end of the hall, upon whose shelves along the walls were arranged learning materials, such as notebooks, pencils, and colored pencils. Miss Stefa was there, waiting for our arrival. We were provided with replacements if we had only a stub of a pencil left, if we had filled up our notebooks, or needed anything else. However, we had to show the old item as proof that we really needed a replacement.

After our "purchases" at the "store," we went down to the cloakroom where we polished our shoes and put on our coats in the winter months, each child taking a coat from his or her own coat hook. Mine was number 43, one of 107.

Holding our school satchels, we proceeded toward the front door where, like a devoted mother, Miss Stefa was again waiting for us. She equipped us with sandwiches for school, which she produced from two large baskets at her side. Understanding the soul of a child, Miss Stefa would vary the fillings of the sandwiches and she was aware of each child's preferences. Usually placing two sandwiches in my hand, she would murmur, "Please, finish them both." Then she would warmly part from us and send us on our way to school.

We felt her constant presence and love, even when she was not physically with us. With silent steps, she would glide around the hall, hurrying from place to place to perform all the many tasks awaiting her. Spotting her out of the corner of our eye, we would gain a feeling of security, knowing that somebody was taking care of us.

At school, we were always identified as Janusz Korczak's children. We were well-kept, quietly behaved, polite, self-confident, and successful at school.

The school was on 61 Grzybowska Street. It was a Jewish state school where we learned general studies together with Jewish history. Studies were conducted in Polish. Most of the teachers were Jewish; Dr. Hecht was the principal of the school. We did not study on Saturdays but we did on Sundays, the Christian Sabbath.

Conflict sometimes arose on our way to and from school. We would walk in groups, for safety's sake. We were accosted by bored Polish children on several occasions, especially on Sundays when they did not attend school. They provoked and abused us, both verbally and physically.

Dr. Korczak was pained by this phenomenon. He repeatedly urged the attackers' parents through the press: "Please, leave my children alone." When the frequency of bullying incidents increased and the staff of the orphanage began to fear for our safety, one of the teachers would accompany us to school, choosing alternative routes for us each time.

At the end of the school day, we returned to the orphanage where a delicious meal awaited us, something different every day.

A happy childhood afternoon

The afternoon hours were filled with hours of pleasure spent through games and activities. We did our homework preparation in the "quiet hall," which was exactly as its name suggests. It was here that we were able read, relax, or rest in a quiet environment. The idea behind this activity was that we were trusted to do our homework. Anybody who required assistance was helped by a teacher who was on duty for that purpose.

After completing our homework, we were free to do anything we wished. For example, we played games. A team of children called "The Group for Beneficial Games" was appointed by the Children's Council. It was responsible for supplying varied equipment for games, such as dominoes, chess, checkers, and ping-pong. We joined two tables from the dining room, drew a net across the center, took out two bats and a ball, and two players were free to engage in an exciting game. During the long winter evenings, we held championships in ping-pong or chess, all intended to benefit our bodies, our souls, and our thoughts.

There was a course for handicrafts and ball games: dodgeball, volleyball, which was extremely popular, and a basketball team called "The Star." These ball games were only played during the summer months when we were able to go out into the yard. During the winter, we were confined indoors.

There were language courses. We could choose Hebrew or Yiddish to preserve our heritage. I chose Esperanto and managed to gain a fairly good mastery of it. There were also courses in history and geography, music, piano, and mandolin. Each child was free to choose whatever subject he or she wished to learn.

There was a large, black, shiny grand piano at the end of the hall on a platform. It was mainly the girls who showed signs of talent and musical ability and they were the ones who played the piano. I also explored my piano playing ability, took several lessons and, well, quite soon I understood that I would never become a pianist. Nobody ever dreamed of disturbing the piano players while they were playing, or approaching the piano if they were not piano students.

The small children received building blocks with which I loved to play and build houses, castles, palaces, and entire cities. If I didn't manage to finish what I was building, I would sometimes leave all the building blocks intact, without tidying them up. Nobody would touch them or move them from their place. Respect and consideration for others was one of the major values instilled in the children at the orphanage.

There was also a sewing course in which I participated. I learned how to mend socks, sew on buttons, and mend tears in clothing.

My favorite pastimes were ping-pong, in which I excelled, and reading. There was a library along one of the walls of the dining room. Its shelves held many adventures and heroes. Once a week, in the evening, we were permitted to borrow books from the library. One of the teachers served as the librarian and advised us which books to read.

During the freezing cold winter months, when winds howled, rains grew torrential, and snow piled up in the streets, covering the trees and the roofs of the houses, I would sit beside the heater where benches were arranged. With piano music in my ears, I was swept into other worlds that opened up before me through the pages of the books.

Each child at the orphanage had a private drawer in which we could store our treasures. I had numerous collections as all children like to keep. My joy was boundless when I had fruit kernels with which to play. I love them to this day. Adults never interfered in these collections unless we asked for assistance. We, the children, had to find our own solutions for our personal or social problems. If one of the adults wanted to guide or advise us, they would say, "If I may say so …"

Playing games with the doctor

Dr. Korczak would sometimes notice that we were bored—or maybe he wished to become a child again. At these times, he would gather us around to play games. One of our favorite games was "The Train." We would file into a long line behind the doctor who was the leader. We would "ride" throughout the entire big house, going in and out of all the halls and rooms, going up and down the stairs, shouts of joy filling all the spaces.

Another game we sometimes played was "Green." Playing "Green" meant that anybody who had any green item in their pockets, such as a leaf or a toy, was the winner.

Playfulness was definitely one of Dr. Korczak's characteristics. He loved to surprise us, catch us unawares, crying: "Now we are going to play 'Green!'" And we immediately pulled out the green items that we always made sure to have in our pockets. Nobody was going to beat us! If we won, Korczak produced a candy from his candy-filled pockets. Even if Korczak had something green in his pocket, it was never revealed and he always lost the game, so we would have our candy prizes.

During the half hour before dinner, we knew that we were required to put away all our games in their proper places. The dining room helpers began to set the tables for dinner.

One of the experiences I remember from the orphanage was in connection with teeth. It is common knowledge that around the age of six, milk teeth start falling out to make place for permanent teeth. A child whose tooth fell out received a coin, which was worth about a half a *zloty*. This was a huge amount for the child who could buy many candies with that money. We all craved that coin and tried to obtain it as fast as possible. If we felt the slightest looseness of a tooth, we ran happily to tell Dr. Korczak about it, "Doctor, my tooth is loose. Is it coming out yet?"

The experienced and wise doctor would pay thoughtful attention to the tooth and then determine, "Not yet, my child. Give it another week. Come back to me and we will check."

The child, obviously disappointed, would go on his way and return impatiently the following week. Again, Dr. Korczak would seriously check the tooth and once again gave his verdict. When the time came for Dr. Korczak to declare that the tooth was ready to leave its home, he would say, "Hmmm, yes, I feel that this time it is much looser." While talking to the child, telling one of his stories to distract him, he would yank the tooth out of its place. Joy! The doctor would fumble in his pockets and pull out the long-awaited coin. Dr. Korczak simply always found a coin in his pocket.

Dr. Korczak's unique method

I wish to tell a very personal story at this point. I stuttered when I was a child. I do not know why, nor do I know when the stuttering began. Ashamed of the fact that I found difficulty in pronouncing words clearly, I shied away from the company of other children. I became sad, irritable, and I felt humiliated.

Obviously, Dr. Korczak and Miss Stefa discerned my problem. Dr. Korczak would never let anything like that escape his perceptive eyes. With Dr. Korczak's agreement, Miss Stefa asked me whether my stuttering bothered me. She then wrote a letter to the school requesting the teachers to refrain from calling me up to the board and to exempt me from any oral testing. I would do all tests in writing, and anything oral would be done in private. Simultaneously, Dr. Korczak called me for a talk and we sat side by side.

"Itzchakeleh," he asked, "Do you want to stop stuttering?"

"Yes."

"I suggest you start out by reading out aloud, by yourself. In that way, you will hear your own voice. Whenever you find a vacant room, enter it, close the door behind you, and sit and read out aloud. Once, twice, three times. If anybody enters the room and interrupts you, stop reading."

I did as he said. I chose books that I liked, and whenever

the opportunity arose, I slipped off into one of the empty rooms, sometimes into the small room that was intended for my painting hobby (I will elaborate upon that later on). I read out aloud, over and over again. What a miracle! When I read to myself, I did not stutter at all.

My explanation for this phenomenon is that, with his calm and quiet manner, Dr. Korczak instilled confidence in me. He understood the soul of a child, he was considerate of my feelings, and he was willing to search for a solution to every child's problems. The general atmosphere of safety at the orphanage also helped me to overcome my stuttering. This was an almost unbelievable solution that did not entail treatments, remonstrations, anger, or humiliation. The only advice I received was, "Sit down and read out aloud to yourself."

Over the years, through persistence, I gradually overcame my stuttering. My gain was threefold. Firstly, I started to speak fluently. Secondly, I was never called up to the blackboard, or asked to speak aloud in front of the whole class, even after my problem had disappeared. The third was that I learned to love reading books, and so it is to this very day.

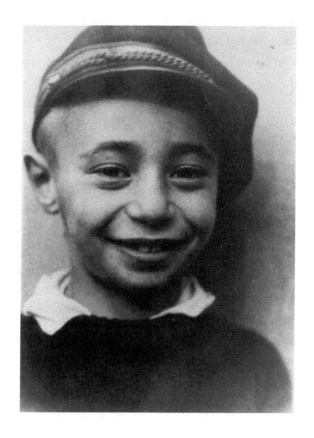

Itzchak - 8 years old at the orphanage

Sabbath traditions

Although the orphanage upheld traditional Jewish values, it was run along secular lines and there was no religious coercion. Friday, the traditional bathing day in Judaism, was the day on which we all bathed at the orphanage. First the girls bathed and then the boys, just before the *Kabbalat Shabbat*.[19] There was no need to urge or remind us or to hurry us up.

You can just imagine a delighted and joyous band of children, chatting, joking, and letting off steam. We were offered the choice of bathing in a bathtub or under a stream of water in a shower. We all chose the shower because it was the most enjoyable. We could play, fool around, splash water, and forget all about the events of the past week. We were all educated to respect each other, not to hurt anyone, and to share our belongings. We were instilled with values of mutual respect.

The doctor was present with us in the bathroom, smiling and inviting everyone to join in the fun. This kind man walked among the young children and patiently, smilingly, taught us how to attend to our personal hygiene. He only allowed us to wash ourselves when he was fully confident that we understood the principles of bathing well enough.

Sweet smelling and dressed in fresh clothes, we ascended to the dining room. Before dinner on Friday nights, one of the children would be waiting in the hall with a hat filled

---

19   Literally "receiving of Shabbat"—a ritual designed to welcome the Jewish Sabbath.

with small notes. These notes bore names of children who, throughout that whole past week, had no complaints filed against them and who had not been defined as "uncaring residents."

Five randomly appointed children pulled out one of these notes, one by one. The five winners constituted the jury for the Children's Court for the coming week. The children posted the list of judges on the bulletin board and the Children's Court was scheduled for nine o'clock on Saturday morning. I was never enthusiastic about becoming a judge or having the responsibility of criticizing my friends, but I was obliged to respect the rules.

The atmosphere on Friday nights was festive. There was a *challah*[20] on each table for the *Kabbalat Shabbat, Shabbat* candles were lit on the central table, and one of our teachers, Jakob Tzuk, blessed the wine. The meal served to the tables was quite different to dinners on any other day of the week. After the meal came the *Oneg Shabbat*.[21] We were told long stories and bedtime was put off for much later.

On Saturday mornings we were woken up late and then we dressed ourselves. After the cod-liver oil ceremony, we were weighed and measured. At the sound of the gong, we sat down quietly for breakfast. There was an assembly of all the orphanage children at 10 a.m.

The assembly took place in the large reading room, each

---

20   Jewish braided bread eaten on the Sabbath and holidays.
21   Literally, "joy of Sabbath," including stories, songs,
         discussions, and refreshments.

child taking his or her chair from the dining room. First, Dr. Korczak reviewed the week by reading from the children's newspaper. The articles in the newspaper were written by the children, while Dr. Korczak had a regular column. The topics of the articles expressed the events of that week. Exceptional cases were discussed, analyzed, conclusions were drawn, and if necessary, we were reprimanded. At the end of this part of the assembly, Miss Stefa read out the verdicts of the judges of the Children's Court.

The Children's Court

The Children's Court was to settle complaints received by any member of the pedagogical staff against any child during the past week. On Saturday mornings, the clerk read out the complaints one by one to the judges, who were the children chosen for that purpose.

The judges discussed the details of each complaint, listened to the various sides of the issues read out to them, and decided upon the appropriate punishment by means of a vote. The punishment was selected from the legal code of the Children's Court, which stressed the value of forgiveness.

Articles 1 to 99 covered minor infractions, pardoned the defendant or even canceled the complaint. The reasoning was: "If the defendant acted wrongly without realizing it, he or she will commit that infraction again in the future. If the defendant committed the act by mistake, he or she will take more care in future. The best action to take is to wait for the child to improve his or her ways."

The next step on the scale of the legal code was for the defendant to be pardoned, but it would be pointed out that he or she acted wrongly. The articles then progressed in units of 100 to 1,000. For example:

Article 100: The court does not declare the defendant guilty, does not censure or display the court's displeasure, but includes the case in the judgment count.

Article 300: You acted wrongly; the court censures this and demands that you do not repeat this action.

Article 600: The court has decided that the defendant was greatly at fault. The judgment must be published both in the newspaper and on the bulletin board.

Article 1000: The child is finally expelled, with the right to apply to the children's Appeals Council for readmission after three months, on condition that the pupil promises to mend his or her ways.

If there was opposition to the verdict, both sides would submit an appeal to the court.

At the end of the assembly, we were free to do as we wished after returning our chairs to their places in the dining room.

General Assembly

The Saturday meal and mother's *kichlach*

Lunch on Saturdays was served at twelve o'clock. I have two memories of these lunches. Firstly, they were quite different from lunch on any other day of the week. Secondly, they included *katchkeleh*, the serving of duck. We loved this dish, which had a distinct taste, the taste of *Shabbat*.

Satisfied after our lunch, those of us who had families or relatives went out to visit their homes at one o'clock. I can still sense the delicious taste of my mother's wonderful *kichlach*[22] which awaited me on Saturdays. They were fresh, crispy, and sweet, just like she was. "How are you, my son?" would be her first question together with a warm kiss. "How do you feel at the orphanage?"

I told her about my new friends, boys and girls, about the events that transpired at school, and about our games. I always finished my account with the words, "Everything is fine, everything is so good there." Mother listened to me, happy to hear what I was telling her, a soft smile on her face, nodding her head. She gave me a hug and a kiss and went on with her work.

The children who remained at the orphanage on Saturday afternoons either joined Dr. Korczak for a walk in the public parks of Warsaw, went to see a film, or ate ice cream.

During the winter, when we were unable to go outdoors, all the children sat around the doctor who read them one of his stories. Indeed, I was sometimes envious of the children

---

22   Yiddish for "cookies"

who remained at the orphanage on Saturday afternoons, for being able to enjoy those activities.

From four o'clock in the afternoon, the orphanage received visits from former pupils who had grown up, left the orphanage, but not forgotten it. These encounters were extremely moving, whether they were among the children, with Dr. Korczak, or Miss Stefa. These orphans had by then married, and brought their wives or families along to these visits to "grandmother and grandfather." They were always met with a huge smile, a hug, a caressing stroke, and an attentive ear.

Those of us who returned early from our visits to our families' homes observed these encounters with curiosity and wonderment, not believing our eyes. Here were small children who had become adults. We did not understand that we, too, were growing and developing.

On Saturday evenings, at about six-thirty, we once again assembled and were served dinner at seven o'clock. We were in our beds at eight o'clock. Lights were extinguished at nine. The next morning we awoke to greet the new week.

Kingdom of the children

During all my years at the orphanage, my peers and I felt sure that this was our home and that we were responsible for its proper management. This was the children's republic. The children were certain that they had both equal rights and duties, all based on the legal code of the orphanage.

The Children's Independent Governing Council was the

highest body in charge of enforcing the legal code of the orphanage. The members of the Children's Council were replaced once a year by elections that lasted for an entire day. The first stage was the election of the parliament, which consisted of twenty children. A child was elected if he or she had the support of five other children of the orphanage. During its first session, the twenty parliament members appointed nine members to constitute the Children's Council. This council appointed the three members of the Court of Appeals and the clerk (an educator) who was, by definition, ineligible for voting.

The Children's Council received a budget of one half a percent of the orphanage income. This sum was deposited into the council's bank account and was used to finance the regular activities of the council and to assist in exceptional cases. The clerk was responsible for depositing the checks into the bank account.

The legal code of the orphanage

The following is an excerpt from the legal code of the orphanage:

- A guardian[23] will be appointed to the new recruit for a period of three months. This period may be shortened or lengthened, according to the needs of both sides. The guardians volunteer for

---

this duty at the general assembly of the children. Boys are in charge of boys and girls are in charge of girls.

- All the children vote to appoint the guardian for the new child from among the candidates. The guardian will provide the child with information, advice, and protection when necessary.

- The guardians will use a notebook to take notes about anything special regarding the new child. At the end of the period of guardianship, the guardian will write down positive and negative traits of the child's behavior from his or her point of view.

- The Children's Court will settle arguments between the new recruit and the guardian.

- A month after the arrival of the new recruit, there will be a referendum regarding the child. Each child in the orphanage receives three notes. One of the notes has a plus sign, meaning that the child votes for the new recruit and another note has a minus sign, meaning that the child does not approve of the new recruit. The third note contains a zero sign, meaning that the child has no opinion or does not care.

- If a child receives a large number of minus signs, he or she will be called a "suspicious recruit" and his or her parents will be notified that their child may be expected to be asked to leave the orphanage.

- A year after the arrival of the new recruit, yet another referendum is held regarding the new child. He or she then receives the status of a "member," a "resident," or a "careless resident," for the negative cases.

- The title that is given by the Children's Independent Governing Council is reexamined each year and is subject to changes.

- The children must study at school or in a group. They must help out by fulfilling their duties. They are obliged to learn Hebrew, gymnastics, singing, and music. Participation in plays and cultural entertainment is not compulsory.

- The Children's Court deals with any arguments between the children and the staff. The court's ruling is according to the legal code. There are 10 convicting sentences, the most severe being expulsion from the orphanage.

- The Children's Court sits once a week. All five judges are appointed each week by drawing lots. Especially important matters are relayed to the Court's Council, consisting of an educator and four children.

- The children visit their families once a week on Saturdays. The Children's Independent Governing Council may grant any child permission for a longer stay at his or her family's home, during holidays or festivals.

- The manager of the orphanage and the chief

educator are responsible to the governing council and the guardian committee for taking care of the children, and are responsible to the children for stringent adherence to the rules of the orphanage.

Dr. Janusz Korczak's room

We all craved a visit to the doctor's room. There was a couch there, waiting only for us. At least, so it seemed to us. It was in that room that could enjoy the undivided attention of Dr. Korczak. What a luxury it was!

It was sufficient to complain of a headache, real or imaginary, for Dr. Korczak to lead us by the hand up the staircase to the room in the attic. Dr. Korczak would place a pillow on the couch, gently lie us down on the couch and caress our brow until we fell asleep, safe and protected.

The room was Spartan in appearance, modestly furnished, with no luxuries or extravagances. On entering, it was the window that first caught one's attention. This arched window exposed a view of Warsaw and below it one could observe the courtyard of the orphanage. The window was composed of connected glass squares. One of the squares, the one closest to the windowsill, resembling a porthole, was always open. This is where the doctor laid two saucers, one filled with water and the other with crumbs of food. "Who was this for?" one may ask. It was for the birds. Every bird of flight was invited for a meal. Dr. Korczak understood the ways of the birds and was an expert in their cycle of life.

There was a large library on the right side of the room behind the couch. On the left was a monastic bed with a mattress and blanket. At the head of the bed, there was a huge desk which Dr. Korczak had inherited from his father. It was constantly covered with books and papers. In addition, the room contained a bench and several chairs and a small mouse that moved around freely, to the delight of the children and the regret of Dr. Korczak's adult guests. The surprising fact is that the mouse never left Dr. Korczak's room to roam around the rest of the house.

It was in this room that the educator Dr. Korczak sat at his large desk, seeking solutions to educational and developmental issues through his unique approach to problems of childhood. It was at this desk that the doctor expressed and composed his pedagogical theories and wrote his books. Besides all of these activities, he created and arranged radio programs in which he administered medical and educational advice to parents. Dr. Korczak would also make notes for lectures he was about to deliver at universities, seminars, Jewish organizations, and the general public.

In his private corner of this room, Dr. Korczak searched for solutions to the economic crisis confronting the entire world, Poland, and the orphanage in particular. Here too, he conceived his ideas for alleviating the lives of the children living under his roof in the orphanage.

Any boy or girl was permitted to visit Dr. Korczak's room for any conceivable physical or emotional reason. Children who had something bothering them or a difficulty of any nature were met with an attentive ear and ample advice. It was here, too, that Dr. Korczak wrote his children's books loved by so many young readers.

Dr. Korczak's numerous projects kept him away from the home during the course of the day for many hours at a time. "I am a father, with all the negative implications of the role," he would say. "I am always busy, with not enough time for leisure. I can tell stories, but I tell them very rarely..."

As soon as the children noticed that Dr. Korczak had returned from his work outside the orphanage, they hurried toward him, clinging to him, hugging him, and being hugged. In return, they received an embrace, a little story, a joke, a smile, or a feeling of security of "daddy has returned home."

Dr. Korczak used games as one of his methods of education. Another method was called "betting." Once a week, at an assigned time, we would find him sitting in the "store," the same room in which we received our school supplies. The purpose of "betting" was to help any child overcome a negative habit that constituted an obstacle in his or her life.

My disobedience, the doctor's bet, and my win

I was an unsociable child. I was ashamed of my stammer, which prevented me from forming relationships and hampered my social bonding with children who, in my opinion, "did nothing." I was boastful of my sports prowess. I sometimes initiated activities that did not receive the cooperation of other children. For a long time, I was merely a "resident" and found

myself involved in arguments, conflict, and fights. I was judged by the Children's Court.

The court found me guilty on several occasions. I so wanted to be recognized as a "member." I usually neglected my studies at school and invested the minimum effort in doing homework assignments. In addition, I was dreamy, absentminded, and created a world of my own.

When I was about eleven years old, I realized that I needed to change certain of my behavior patterns in order to become socially accepted. I sought the advice of the doctor, certain that he was able counsel and instruct me.

A long queue formed outside the "store" on the assigned day. I waited impatiently in the line for my turn to talk to the doctor. When my turn finally arrived, Dr. Korczak asked, "How can I help you?"

"I am ashamed of my negative behavior toward the other children."

"I agree with you. It is important that you change your attitude. But please know, my child, this is going to be a long and difficult process. You will succeed if you show persistence and determination. Now please tell me, how many times a week will be enough for you to argue and fight?"

"None at all."

"You may argue and fight no more than four times a week. Obviously, you should try to stay out of confrontations, and do not accumulate more than two court cases a week." I received a candy as a sign of agreement. "Come back to me in a week's time and we will see whether you have succeeded."

I returned to him.

"How was it?" he asked.

"Not very successful, I think. I was arrogant this week and I was involved in more than four fights."

"Never mind," said the doctor who knew that I had made an honest effort, and that I was trying. "That was the first week. From now on, not more than four times."

This is how, from week to week, I continued the process. Success was met with two candies. Failure meant a new agreement and only one candy.

The process finally succeeded, thanks to Dr. Korczak's patience and tolerance. It took me a long time, during which I learned to be less boastful, to make friends with the children, respect others, not to interrupt through an assumption that I knew better, and in short, to be more considerate of others.

I had learned an important lesson: One must be persistent and unrelenting in order to succeed. Life is preferable in a supportive and accepting environment. I eventually earned the title of "member" and I indeed felt that I belonged.

I became an artist in this home

Miss Stefa approached me one day when I was about ten years old. Placing a warm hand on my shoulder, she said, "Itzchakeleh, I know that you love drawing. If you wish, I will give you pages, pencils, colors, paintbrushes, and anything else you need. You may take the key to the 'store' from the office whenever you like. This will be your very own corner where you will be able to sit quietly and draw."

My joy knew no bounds. My dream to draw was materializing. The excitement that swept me improved my self-esteem. I surmised that if Miss Stefa knew about my talent for drawing, the doctor probably knew too.

As an adult, I am able to appreciate the attention and perception of the doctor and Miss Stefa toward each of the children at the orphanage. There were 170 children in the home, each consisting of a world of its own, bearing different characters, personalities, and talents. Both Dr. Korczak and Miss Stefa succeeded in identifying and cultivating the hidden talents and strong points of each and every one of us, despite all the menial tasks they performed and the day-to-day problems and obstacles that required solutions. The doctor and Miss Stefa recognized our weak points too. They directed and guided us.

Until that point, I had been satisfied with sketching in my school notebook. But now I was equipped with a drawing pad, gouache paints, pencils, and pencil crayons for coloring, all of which allowed my imagination to run wild.

I have no doubt that the attention and guidance that I received from the doctor and Miss Stefa facilitated my affinity to the visual arts. The small room at my disposal was a private and quiet haven in which I could develop my talents and engross myself in books and dreams. I committed the drawings I had created in my imagination to paper using a pencil and paintbrush. I painted many landscapes, whether real or imagined.

Neither the doctor nor Miss Stefa ever visited me in my small room. They had full confidence in me and did not need to check on me. I did not tell anybody at home that I had started to draw.

Camp once again, at the start of summer

How many children, especially children of an orphanage, had the privilege of attending summer camp during those years? We, the children of the orphanage, enjoyed this luxury because we had the distinguished Dr. Korczak, who understood how the human soul craved freedom, change, and refreshment. He was the person who sought to pamper us with the joys of nature.

Our school closed its gates when the summer heat began, and we were sent off on vacation. We set out excitedly and expectantly for the camp on a farm in Goclawek, a short distance away from Warsaw. We traveled first by tram and then by horse and cart, announcing our arrival with jubilant singing.

As soon as we arrived at our destination, we excitedly ran barefoot toward the golden spans of sand, surrounded by green fields. The reason for running like that was to claim our stakes to our private little corners of land. Each of us took possession of a little plot of sand and immediately started digging sand holes, a meter deep, a meter wide, with wooden logs serving as steps to the bottom of our new dwellings, using tree branches for a roof. We were careful to mark out the borders of our territory in which we could escape from everybody else, or else to invite friends to come and play or talk. We always found topics of interest to discuss.

Dr. Korczak stayed on throughout our holiday at Go-clawek and succeeded in giving us a feeling of freedom through organized games, maintaining a high level of mutual respect between us at all times. After breakfast, we were free as birds. Barefoot and wearing light clothing, we charged around in the open spaces.

Some of us spread our wings and went out to inspect the green fields. Others joined the doctor for walks in the nearby forest, burrowing and searching for treasures in the dark shadows of the trees—blackberries, mushrooms, interesting leaves, and a pebble for a souvenir, a squirrel to which to say good morning, or a dried fruit that had fallen from one of the trees. The older children enjoyed the privilege of paid employment in the farm's hothouses. I picked fruit and, like my friends, earned ample money to be able to buy several luxuries for myself on our return to Warsaw.

In the afternoons, after scrubbing off all evidence of the morning's activities, we gathered once again in the dining room. Dr. Korczak was consistent in educating us about our own personal hygiene.

We occupied ourselves during our leisure time in the afternoons playing table games, outdoor games, simply running wild, or practicing for the "Olympic Games" that were held at the beginning of the second month of our stay at the camp. Hungry and thirsty after these activities, we were served sandwiches, fruit, and water in the dining room.

Even here, in the dining room, Dr. Korczak provided us with an important lesson in life. Above the dining table there

was a poster indicating that we should eat and enjoy ourselves, but that we should make sure to leave enough for the other children.

At the end of the day's activities, we sat down for dinner washed, combed, and dressed in fresh clothes. After dinner, we gathered around the doctor, listening to his stories, talking about everyday matters, making requests, and solving problems.

Among the numerous activities of the camp were occasional excursions in which we learned about new places. One of our favorite outings was to the Vistula River, the climax of which was the inevitable prank that the doctor played, which usually reduced us to tears of laughter.

A moment of grace

I was about twelve years old, still small and thin. I awoke one morning at the summer camp to the sound of whispering voices. Dr. Korczak and Miss Stefa were standing at the foot of my bed with a concerned countenance. "Itzchakeleh, are you feeling all right?" asked Miss Stefa. "Are you hungry? Should I bring you something to eat?" I was late waking up that morning, and like two concerned parents, they were worried that something was wrong with me. Nothing was the matter with me. I was simply in the deep sleep of an adolescent.

"There is no need to bring me anything to eat," I answered, embarrassed at the concern I had aroused. "Everything is all right, I will eat when I get up."

"In that case, continue sleeping as much as you like," said

Miss Stefa, stroking my head.

I will never forget that heartwarming moment, a moment of love and concern.

Dr. Korczak regarded physical exercise as paramount to our well-being. He held "Olympic Games" at the camp to encourage us to train and strive for excellence. The games were organized for all the children at the camp by the Committee for Beneficial Games. The sports included athletics, high jump, long jump, and team games.

Sports games were for boys and girls together and some of them were for boys or girls separately. There were three stages for each sport—quarterfinals, semifinals, and final, as in the real world.

I was small and nimble and participated in the long-distance running competitions, 400 and 800 meters. I sometimes came first in these competitions. I also enjoyed competing in the well-being team. As an older child, I was even selected as the captain of the volleyball team.

There were also fun games, such as the sack race in which we ran with our legs in a sack tied at our waists, the egg and spoon race, in which we ran while holding an egg in a spoon, the loser being the first one to drop the egg, and a tug-of-war competition.

After the sports day we, of course, slept very soundly.

Participation in the sports events taught us to strive for excellence and to practice seriously for these competitions. These lessons proved to be useful tools later in our independent adult lives.

Tonight is the big night

During the evening meal, the boys were flooded with a wave of concern that the girls could get wind of the boys' plans for a nocturnal walk on the sands that night. The boys went to bed earlier than usual, excited and barely able to fall asleep.

At midnight, we silently crept out of our beds and rooms, cautious not to let any noise awaken the girls. Dressed in warm clothing and carrying potatoes for the camp fire, we set out into the cold night in the direction of the forest with the doctor and a teacher on duty.

The further we moved from the farmhouse, the louder our cries of joy. Our laughter and animated singing drove away any apprehensions about going off to seek an adventure.

After walking for about a half hour, we reached the forest, prepared to experience the climax of the camp's activities.

Twigs released sparks of fire and snapping sounds from the camp fire we lit. Our appetites were aroused by the smell of the potatoes, the *kartoshkes*, roasting away, trapped between the whispering coals. We sat around the fire on blankets spread out on the ground, bewitched and amused by Dr. Korczak's tales.

The exhilaration of that night made way for fatigue. Still smiling with happiness, the younger children fell asleep and the older ones stayed awake, taking turns at guard duty.

At the crack of dawn, we returned to the farmhouse, proud, merry and noisy, waking up the girls with our shrieks of laughter, and arousing their envy of our night's adventure. Needless to say, the girls were also treated to such a night on another occasion!

We were permitted to carry on sleeping until lunchtime the following morning, obviously not before we had cleaned ourselves of everything that had adhered to our clothes and bodies during our hike and campfire.

We cherished this experience. Recollections of the nocturnal picnic of the Goclawek camp are still vivid in my memory.

At the end of August, our splendid summer vacation finished, and we returned home to the orphanage in Warsaw, full of energy and equipped with a sack full of memories and experiences.

Korczak Znany i Nieznany
(Korczak Known and Unknown)

By Professor Aleksander Lewin,[24]
translated by Yitzhak Belfer

When I first stepped into the orphanage, I felt as though I was in a strange, interesting, and unknown land, totally different from what I had been used to until then. Some of the children were playing in the courtyard in front of the building and others were setting the tables for dinner in the dining room.

The children's behavior was confident and assured. Their faces showed that they were serious, smiling, and prepared to help. They immediately displayed an interest in the new person who had come to work with them. During the communal meal, they proudly and patiently explained everything regarding the ways and customs of the house, the dining room, homework preparation, the weekly newspaper, family visits, and sleeping arrangements.

This was the beginning of my training as an educator. I first received verbal guidance and later acquired practical experience at the orphanage. I learned all the about the system from within.

---

24   Professor Lewin was my teacher from 1937–1938. During the time he was employed at the orphanage, he was still a student. We met again after the war and formed a close friendship that lasted for many years. Above is a quotation from his book. (Y.B.)

Paradoxically, it was the children and not the doctor or Miss Stefa who introduced me to the everyday routine and the important rules of the orphanage. From the first moment I started working there until I left, I had the distinct feeling that the children held some kind of secret regarding the rules and legal code of the house. There were so many rules and regulations that one could easily go astray, but not the children. It happened to Dr. Korczak, to Miss Stefa, but never to the children.

CHAPTER 3:

No Longer a Child

"There are no children, just people who have different ranges of understanding, experiences, desires, and feelings. Remember! We do not know them."

- Janusz Korczak

I stood alone at a crossroads for the first time in my life—sad, afraid, bewildered, and helpless. According to the legal code of the orphanage, I was to leave at the end of my elementary school studies. I was fourteen years old and the time for my departure was drawing near.

Where would I go? What would I do? There was no room for me at home. My mother was worn-out due to her strenuous life, having barely enough money to support the family. How could I impose myself upon her? My *yiddishe*[25] childhood lifestyle had already become foreign to me. I felt

---

alienated. I had developed and been exposed to distant, different, and interesting worlds. I did not have a profession, so where would I find employment? It was clear to me that as a boy from a poor home living in those times, I would have no choice but to go out and work once I finished my studies at elementary school. Time was running out, but still I had no solution.

"Itzchak," said Miss Stefa, as she called me in those days instead of "Itzchakeleh," another sign that I was growing up, "I know what you are going through. I also know what your family's situation is at home. Why don't you put in a request to the Children's Council to stay at the orphanage for another year? You should state in your request that if the council agrees, you will commit yourself to any assistance that may be required, in the house, or in caring for the children."

I felt an immediate sense of relief. I drafted a letter in which I gave all my reasons for requesting an additional year at the orphanage and my pledge to be of assistance in any way I could. After several days, I received a positive answer to my request.

In retrospect, I understand now as an adult that Miss Stefa and Dr. Korczak had initiated this move to help me out of my predicament. As a young boy, it was so wonderful that the children, in this case the Children's Council, was authorized to discuss requests, consider facts, and make decisions.

My first employment

The secretariat of the orphanage was responsible for finding me employment. I am sure that Miss Stefa was involved in this issue, thanks to the connections and respect that she and Dr. Korczak had cultivated. The job was at a well-known and prestigious record store in Warsaw, owned by Jews. Radio Poland even purchased records for its broadcasts from that store.

I was proud and excited. I, Itzchak, already a grown boy, was working and earning money as a messenger boy. I was responsible for delivering vinyl records that had been ordered by wealthy and respected Warsaw residents. I extremely enjoyed the task! I would often save the tramway fare and walk through the streets of Warsaw, looking around me curiously, drinking in the sights and sounds, taking my time and not always in a hurry to reach my destination. After two weeks, the storeowner suggested that I buy myself a bicycle. "Your deliveries are too slow. A bicycle will save you time and you will be able to make more deliveries," she said.

I consulted with Miss Stefa. "Why don't you submit a request to the Children's Council?" she said. I put in a request, which was approved on condition that two council members accompany me to purchase the bicycle. Of course I agreed. When I relate this story today, I smile to myself. My companions were younger than me and the business of purchasing and selling items was foreign to them. The orphanage treated us so wonderfully, giving us the feeling that we were grown-up, responsible, respected, and able to reflect and make decisions, to feel independent and as though we were prepared for adult life.

On a pre-arranged day, we set out for a bicycle repair store. In a very adult manner, we had decided to buy the parts for assembling a bicycle on our own instead of purchasing a new bicycle. There was no happier person than me. My joy was boundless! I pedaled away proudly and happily, sailing through the streets of Warsaw!

The days went by, weeks, and months. I was floating on a cloud. I was the owner of a bicycle, working, earning a wage, and returning to sleep at the orphanage in the evenings.

And then it happened. Somebody coveted the bicycle. It was not even new or shiny. It was worth nothing. But it was mine. One day, on the way back from a delivery, I tied the bicycle to its regular place at the back entrance of the store. When I was called to my next delivery, my heart missed a beat. The bicycle was not there anymore, as if it had never been there. I went back to the store but was so tearful and upset that I could barely articulate the words: "Somebody took my bicycle." I could not believe it had happened.

I told Miss Stefa what had happened. I felt betrayed. How could anybody steal a bicycle that three innocent children had assembled so painstakingly?

Miss Stefa had foreseen what was about to happen and, unbeknownst to me, had already started looking for another place of employment for me. About one week after the theft, I was indeed fired from my job as a messenger at the record store. Thanks to that kind and wise woman, the mother of all the orphans, I was hired as an apprentice in a small enterprise that assembled radios. It was called Trio Radio and was also under Jewish ownership. The company was located on Grzybowska Street, a stone's throw away from the Jewish school where I had been a pupil.

The time was drawing close for me to leave the orphanage, the home of Dr. Korczak and Miss Stefa. "Itzchak," said Miss Stefa, "You will be returning to your home in several days. This is a new chapter in your life. You will receive a suitcase containing full sets of clothes, from head to toe. We bid you the best of luck."

Once again, I stood before the iron gate of the tall brick wall. This time, I was on the other side of it, and I was alone. I left the home holding a suitcase. I was leaving the courtyard and leaving my childhood years behind. A click of the latch and I was on the outside.

In all honesty, I remember nothing of the process of parting. I do not remember the hours before I left, or whether anybody accompanied me. Were they watching me from behind? I do not remember the very moment at which my feet stepped outside the orphanage.

All I remember is how extremely trying it was to return to my mother's home. Chaya, my older sister, was still living at home. She and my mother welcomed me with warm and loving embraces, which gave me the feeling that I was wanted there. Although it was, in fact, my home, I felt strange and detached. It was difficult to readapt to life in my mother's home.

The physical conditions and economic situation dampened my spirits. Five of us were crammed into one room. My mother barely made a living, and I was an adolescent boy who naturally required independence and privacy. I was a little envious of my older brothers who had already married and set up their own homes. However, I had no choice or alternative solution.

During all of those days I carried on working at Trio Radio, which was a haven for me. The work was mechanical and repetitious, consisting of transporting the framework of the radio from one worker to another for assembly, in a sort of conveyer belt. One worker added a part; I transferred it to the next worker who, in turn, added a component, and so on. I loved watching the process and also managed to learn the principles of radio assembly.

The highlight of the process was a visit to the room in which the engineers inspected the finished product. It was an apparent miracle when the radio began to work and emit sounds and voices. On several occasions, at the end of the day's work on my way home, I would stop for a minute or two near the wall of the orphanage, listening for any sounds that might be coming out of there, imagining the activities going on inside, feeling nostalgia, and then stepping away with a heavy heart.

From a secure home to reality

Injuries and harm to the Jewish population were, at that time, becoming routine. The first event of that nature that I witnessed left me shocked and distressed.

It was a summer's evening and I was on my way from work to my mother's home. Reaching the Polish quarter, I heard shouts of anger and hatred. "*By Żydzi!* Hit the Jews, hit them!"

The voices became louder and came nearer to where I was standing. The uproar of stamping feet indicated a huge crowd. I heard shouts of pain and crying. I stayed near a wall of one of the buildings, as did other people around me, hoping not to be noticed and wishing to miraculously become invisible.

The crowd passed me by. Hundreds of people were bearing sticks and batons in their hands and were insanely screaming instructions to hit the Jews. I could not fathom the source of this savagery.

Luckily for me, I escaped the crowd's notice, as I resembled a Pole rather than a Jew, in both appearance and dress. After many moments, my breathing went back to normal and finally I dared to leave my temporary shelter. My knees shaking, I returned home, trying to understand what I had just witnessed.

It was only much later that I was conscious of the painful understanding that the rabble was collaborating with the pro-Nazi Polish government in the incitement of the mob against the Jews.

Like many other graduates of the orphanage, I participated in the gatherings that took place on Saturdays. During one of these gatherings, I conversed with two of my friends and we realized that we were in the same situation. We discussed the difficulty of living under the same roof as the family on the one hand, and bearing the financial burden of independent lodgings on the other. We decided to take action and to rent an apartment together.

We rented an apartment from a Jewish family in the Jewish quarter. We shared the kitchen, bathroom, and toilet with the family. Life began to seem brighter to me. We each left the apartment in the morning for work and in the evenings we spent time together and we had independent lives. We wove dreams together, made plans, enjoyed ourselves in the company of girls, and planned our futures.

Friday,
9.1.1939

The beginning of the horrendous war

When Warsaw was bombed for the first time and shells threatened to hit its buildings, we ran back to our families' homes as fast as we could, so we could be with the others. My two brothers and their families also came to my mother's home, each couple cradling their baby. We sat together, fearful of what was about to happen. Together we hoped and prayed for the best.

The shortage of food worsened. There was no water and no electricity. Day and night, we ran for shelter at the wailing of the sirens. Fear crept in and we were restless. Heavy shelling and airplane bombing shattered Poland to pieces. The Polish air force was destroyed and the Germans, having the upper hand, increased the pressure.

Toward the end of the month

The war that shocked the entire world and the Jewish people was already in full swing. It was then that an incident occurred which rocked our whole family, and left me sorrowful and aching. The bombing and shelling subdued Poland and she surrendered to the Germans. The German army appeared at the gates of Warsaw in an aggressive victory march.

My family and I gathered in the streets with many of our neighbors and the general population of Warsaw. Anxious masses of people were waiting outside their homes. Who knew what awaited us?

My grandfather's house was at the edge of the city. My grandparents sat close to the wall of the house. My mother, brother, sister, and I were standing beside them. Several meters separated us from the road. A German military vehicle appeared suddenly, driving slowly, and stopped opposite us. Two Germans, an officer and a soldier, emerged from the vehicle. They slowly crossed the small wooden bridge leading to the house and approached us with evil smiles on their faces. An unpleasantly cold laugh replaced their smile.

One of the soldiers grabbed my grandfather's beard, pulling him to his feet. The other took out a large pair of scissors, and began to cut off his beard, all the while laughing gleefully. The locks of hair started falling down, piling up at their feet. They carried on with their task, cutting precisely, taking care to cut only one side of the beard, all the while laughing hysterically. They were in no hurry, taking pains to enjoy what they were doing, and drew out their entertainment. When one half of my grandfather's beard was fully shaved, the soldiers retreated, entered the vehicle and left, their evil laughter still echoing in our ears and chilling our hearts.

We remained transfixed and almost paralyzed. Dumbfounded, humiliated, and helpless, we could not grasp what our eyes had beheld. We were convinced that these messengers of the devil were simply stopping by our house to ask for directions.

Supported by my grandmother and mother, my grandfather dragged his feet toward the house, and closed himself in his room, refusing to see anyone except my grandmother. We were trembling and confused, having never witnessed such cruelty before.

We tried to console our grandfather and calm him down, but his bedroom door remained locked before us. My grandfather's pain could not be alleviated and he permitted my grandmother only to enter and to bring him small portions of food and drink.

After several days, when my grandfather finally came out of his room, he was unrecognizable. Grandfather, the hero of my childhood, had once been an upright, bearded, well-groomed, and good-looking man who carried his age gracefully; courageous in his actions and thoughts. Instead, out of the room emerged an old man, his face shaven, wrinkled, his eyes extinguished. He looked small, bent, downcast, with a slow and weary gait, as though he bore a heavy load on his shoulders—the burden of being Jewish.

Shocked and aching, the family unanimously decided to move away from our home. My uncle, my mother's oldest brother, and his wife were living in an apartment in the Jewish quarter of Warsaw. For some reason or other, there were several vacant apartments in their building. Their residents had possibly sought refuge somewhere else, owing to the raging war.

We moved into one of the vacant apartments in the Jewish quarter. Since we were, at that time, required to wear Star of David armbands signifying that we were Jewish, we thought that we would be better off residing in a Jewish neighborhood, where we lived in a community.

After a short time, I arrived at my place of employment, Trio Radio, only to find the premises locked and a notice reading: "Trio Radio has closed, due to the war." What was I to do? How would I make a living? How would I help my mother? I was immersed in desperation. The days of my youth were over.

There was a dire shortage of food by then. Enterprises were closing down or sending their products to the Germans, and stores were sealed up. The ones that remained open had only a few products to offer. Fortunately, my uncle was the owner of a bakery so we at least had bread—and I had a job for a short while.

My uncle suggested that I join the group of peddlers and sell bread rolls in the makeshift market that had sprung up in one of the streets. Bread was always in demand. I walked around and sold my wares, carrying a pail of rolls in addition to a wooden tray of rolls that was tied around my neck by a strip of leather.

When I felt tired, I laid the pail on the street corner, placed the tray on top of it, and continued my sales from there. People bought my rolls and I made a little money for our upkeep.

One morning, my route was blocked by a group of Jewish street children. They flanked me from three sides, stole all my rolls and ran away. This was the last time I went out to sell rolls.

I had a new job offer. One of my friends sold books in the street. Interestingly, despite the hardships, people were thirsty for books in order to temporarily escape from reality and enter the lives of other, imaginary people. A book publisher was looking for salespeople. A friend of mine recommended me and I was offered the job. I sold light novels in Polish mainly to Jewish people. I do not remember how successful I was at this job as I am unable to remember why I stopped selling books.

From this point on, I concentrated my efforts on finding food for my family, and bringing water to our home. The authorities opened water distribution stations at various public places in Warsaw. I used to visit one of these stations holding a pail in each hand and waiting for a long time in the queue for my turn to fill the pails at the faucets. Then I would return home, careful not to let any of the water spill out of the pails. When the precious water reached its destination I went out again to stand in yet another queue, this time for food.

The search for food around the streets of Warsaw was an extremely difficult task, which I carried out without the armband signifying my shame, my being Jewish. I trusted that my "Warsawian" appearance and blue eyes would not betray my true origin. Wandering around a Christian area with an armband would have been, at best, an invitation to be beaten, and in the worst case, shot to death.

I strode long distances through the streets, merely to find a store with one can of preserves on its shelves, or another store with a small amount of beans. If I was fortunate, I would perhaps find a handful of noodles or potatoes, cabbage, cauliflower, or a beet or two. Any find would satisfy me, anything that would stave off our grueling hunger.

My walks through Warsaw took me to the neighborhood of my childhood. I hoped that I would find some fruit in the fields at the back of the church opposite our old house. Many others had the same idea, mainly Christians. They were also starving and there was very little left for anybody to find.

The Nazis were aware of the starvation that had smitten Warsaw. Sometimes a truck would stop across the road and soldiers would throw out round loaves of old and dry black bread to the crowds that gathered in their tens or hundreds. This was mainly to show "consideration" and "humanity" before the movie cameras that filmed the "gesture" for purposes of propaganda. One can easily imagine the commotion, the shoving, and shouting. Everybody stretched out their arms to catch a loaf. While the Germans found this sight entertaining, it was, for us, an opportunity to bring home some food to eat. I was sometimes successful too. Mother would then cover the loaf with a damp cloth, to restore some of its softness, and of course we all shared the bread down to its last crumb.

Aktions **(Abductions)**

Several months after the occupation of Warsaw, the Germans began to round up the Jews into one residential area, the Jewish quarter, later known as the Warsaw Ghetto. Jews all over Warsaw were ordered to exchange their homes with Poles. The *Judenradt*, or Jewish Council, paid a high ransom for postponing the date of implementing the final demarcation of the ghetto. Even before the ghetto gates were finally locked and movement to other areas of Warsaw was still permissible, the authorities began to build a three-meter wall covered with barbed wire. The overcrowded conditions inside worsened from day-to-day and several families had to occupy a single apartment. Violators of the curfew were severely punished.

The Nazis were known for the *aktions* they organized. The German word *aktion* means "action" or "campaign"— although we already knew by then that the word embodied the action of locating, arresting, and deporting Jews. We were, at that stage, under the impression that Jews were being sent to forced labor camps. I was witness to these *aktions* on several occasions, when the Germans closed the streets, blocked off any escape routes, and abducted Jews.

One evening, I was hurrying to get home before the curfew, after seeking food all day. When I was already inside the ghetto, I was caught in an *aktion*.

We were driven in two trucks about 30 kilometers east of Warsaw, to a labor camp. Our task was to clear out wreckage and dig a security ditch. The work was arduous and crushing, and we worked from sunrise to sunset without a moment's rest, with no water or food. When we returned to the camp in the evenings, we were given a bowl of thin soup.

On our discharge from the labor camp on the third morning, we formed into groups to plan our way back home. To avoid capture, we chose a route through forests, moving by night and resting by day, to avoid residential areas. Despite our starvation and exhaustion, I managed to return home to my family two days later, to my mother who had lost sleep through concern for my safety. My mother asserted that her strength would not hold out for another event like the last one and that we had to find a solution. I agreed with her and we decided to find a way of escape out of that hell.

Never imagining that it would take another five years for the infernal war to be over, the idea of escape seemed reasonable. Naïve and hopeful, I believed that life would return to normal after a short time, and that I would soon return to my home.

A blessing from the doctor

I encountered one of my friends during one of my Saturday visits to the orphanage. From our conversation, I understood that, like me, he wished to escape the pressure and persecution of life in Warsaw. There was a prevalent rumor that it was safe to reside in a Polish area occupied by the Russians about 100 kilometers from Warsaw. We decided to cross the border to Bialystok, which was the closest city on our escape route. In truth, we did not think too far ahead. The main consideration was to depart from the ghetto and live elsewhere. We imagined that after several months, we would return to Warsaw.

Our anxious and concerned families were resigned to our decision and gave us their blessing without hesitation. We wished for the blessing of Dr. Korczak as well.

The situation in the orphanage was severe. The number of children residing there was now 150 girls and boys, some of whom were war orphans. Money was lacking, food was rationed, and it was difficult to heat the rooms adequately. The building was in need of repair since it had been damaged by the shelling. Above all, fear of eviction was hovering over their heads. Since Krochmalna Street was located in the Christian quarter, Dr. Korczak was commanded to evict the building and move the children to the Jewish quarter, which became the ghetto.

We found the doctor in the large hall surrounded by a circle of children, talking to them quietly. We apologized for interrupting them and explained the purpose of our visit. I will never forget the silent, shocked, and tense atmosphere. Tears welling in his kind and wise eyes, the doctor said these chilling words that have remained with me forever, "The nestlings are departing. They are flying from their nest."

The kind man, knowing us as a father, expressed total understanding. The doctor himself had been imprisoned for refusing to wear the armband. He had always opposed any type of coercion, and his educational doctrine encouraged free thought and respect for others. Having no other choice, the doctor gave us his blessing, provided us with several useful tips, and placed some small change into our hands.

This was the last time I ever saw Dr. Korczak and Miss Stefa, who was standing to one side. I am not sure whether she participated in the conversation or not. She possibly remained silent due to her inability to help.

A Letter to Dr. Janusz Korczak

In my old age, I wish to thank you on behalf of all the children of the Janusz Korczak orphanage. I wish to express my deep respect and esteem for your most supreme work in which you educated desperate orphan children toward the undisputed belief in the struggle for the rights and respect of the child.

You were full of love for children and concern for humanity. You educated us toward honesty, fairness, work, and mutual respect. Thanks to your education methods at the orphanage, we fully understood the meaning of freedom and equalitarian, democratic education.

The Children's Court operated for the benefit of all and the legal code of our home was identical for everyone, including staff members. The Children's Council was fully involved in decisions of the management and in the daily routine of the orphanage.

Your educational doctrine proved to be successful in two orphanages and in many other institutions. You adhered to your doctrine even in the worst of times, during the war, and in the ghetto.

My deepest thanks and respect for granting us a

happy childhood, filled with significant experiences, light, color, and joy.

It was my honor to live in your midst, to be nourished by your wisdom, and enjoy your warmth.

Thank you for laying the foundations of the warm home you built for us. You showed us the way without ever expecting anything in return.

You were selfless in your sensitive, loyal, and loving care of us.

You taught us to love others, and that there is no love without forgiveness.

You instilled in us hope for a better life someday, a life of truth and justice.

You showed us the path to the Land of Israel and it is here that we have found the love of mankind and the Homeland.

We remember you with reverence.
We will cherish your memory forever.

Itzchak Belfer,
a Child of the Orphanage

To Itzchak Belfer

Your teacher was the best of our times; he was like a father,
Your visions of childhood under his patronage were like a gold mine.
You remember a light blue smile with a murmur of longing.
When you speak of him, pain penetrates the hearts of the listener …

"The children who grew up there were privileged," you tell your students,
"The doctor would say this …"
All the details of your experiences are instilled in others.
They feel his presence, indeed these events really happened,
Your stories bring him back, like a resurrection.

You were born gifted, an artist,
Your eyes fill with tears, but your stories are so joyful.
This artist is a Jew and that is another of his traits.
He immigrated to Israel to create his art in the land of his forefathers.

The man's testimony is both the topic and his mission,
Day and night, he bears the painful memory of the Holocaust of his people,
With unending love and a stroke of a brush, he creates and documents the events that he witnessed.

I observe you, Itzchak, while you are at work.
I see you among the children, listen to your stories.
I watch how your smile sheds a tear which then dries up,
And you in your Warsaw childhood can run and play once again ...

Bless you, kind Itzchak, we are all certain that Dr. Korczak is here with you today.
He, too, bestows his blessing upon you.

The poetess Yardena Hadas

CHAPTER 4:

Path of Survival

"How much do we as adults need to educate ourselves in order to understand children? It is not enough to love children. You need to understand them and treat them as human beings. Give them the same rules, rights and obligations by which adults must abide."

- Janusz Korczak

The end of 1939

I set out the next day, after an emotional farewell from my mother and the rest of my family. Carrying knapsacks containing clothing, food, and money, my companion and I boarded the east-bound train traveling to Malkinia, the closest town to the Russian border. The train was crowded with passengers: German soldiers, Polish citizens and bearded Jewish evacuees, wearing the armband of disgrace. With adolescent arrogance, my companion and I removed our identification armbands before entering the coach.

The train whistled, the engine hummed and thundered, the wheels rumbled, and the train was on its way. Germans, joined by the Poles, gleefully began to harass the evacuees by provoking them, pushing their children around, grabbing belongings from them, mocking them, and playing a cruel game of the strong against the weak. The masters of the land against the displaced people, uprooted from their homes.

We sat wrapped up on seats at the side, trying our best to remain inconspicuous. We felt their suspicious glances upon us, wondering about our identities.

Our discomfort became fear of impending danger. It would be disastrous if our true identities were disclosed there, closed up in the train with no way of escape. The situation became unbearable. Whispering to each other, we decided to get off the train at the very next station, whatever the case.

We were only halfway to our final destination when we disembarked from the train and were able to breathe freely again. Fortunately, we remained unnoticed since the station was a remote one. We ran for dear life, making sure to keep far away from any settlement, and continued through the forests. We knew we would have to walk by night and rest by day. Here we were, two inexperienced urban Jewish boys, lost in unfamiliar territory, outwardly courageous, but supporting each other through mutual encouragement.

Plagued with hunger, we began to walk along the railroad tracks to keep going in the right direction. The little food we had brought from home was gone. We searched for wild fruit and berries or anything we could find. We were thirsty and petrified.

Fatigue overcame us on our third day of walking. Anxious that we would not have the strength to continue, we decided to leave the forest and search openly for food. From a distance, we saw a line of people headed eastwards, in the same direction as us. Although we did not know who these people were, we decided to join them. When we approached them, we identified them as Jewish and Polish evacuees. We were, for a moment, relieved, but later understood that this was a column led by Germans. Anybody daring to leave it was shot. We found ourselves among them. We had no choice and could not turn back.

The column stopped at Malkinia, which is located near Treblinka. The town center was partially fenced off. The Germans began their selection or *selektzia*, a word whose association in the German context strikes everyone with terror. The Germans released the Poles, but confined entire Jewish families to the closed area. Our turn had arrived.

"You," said the German, pointing to me, "are free." He pushed me out with the butt of his rifle. "And you," he roared at my friend. "Go there, with all the Jews." I resembled a Pole and remained alive.

I hurriedly left town, looking for a route that would lead me to the forest in which to hide while I walked in the direction of the border. My aim was to cross the border and seek refuge.

I chose a dirt path and began to walk. After a while, I heard the sound of wheels and horse hooves approaching. My heart skipped a beat. The cart overtook me, stopped, and the cart driver, a Polish farmer, asked, "Young man, where are you headed?"

"To the border," I replied.

"But the border is far away. Come and sit beside me and I will take you some of the way." We traveled quite a long way together in the cart.

"Do you know where the border is?" he asked me.

"No. There," I said, pointing in a general direction. Again silence.

I did not know whether he was to be trusted, whether he would turn me in to the Germans.

"Do you have any money?" he asked. "If you do, I can help you. Would you like that?" I certainly required his assistance.

The Polish man brought me to his home, sat me at his table, and his wife served me a large plate of the best food. How tasty were the piece of meat and *kluskies*![26]

I devoured everything on my plate as only a starving person can do, without leaving a single crumb. I received a second serving and finished that off as well. While I was eating, the Polish couple spoke quietly to each other.

"Look," the man eventually said to me. "Our house is isolated here in the field. The forest is nearby and the Germans are searching for collaborators here too. If they find you, we are doomed. I will take you to the barn where you can hide and from there I will lead you to the border. But let's first make a deal. How much money do you have?"

I told him how much I had.

"Give it to me."

---

26   Polish dumplings made of flour and cheese.

"But I must leave some money for myself," I attempted to say.

He took almost all of my money, went through my knapsack and took whatever he could. Satisfied, he led me to the barn and hid me deep inside a pile of hay.

I heard voices of Germans carrying out a search during the night. They did not detect me, and the voices faded as the Germans retreated.

The farmer stood beside me. "Young man, tonight is too bright a night and we cannot leave now. Stay here. We will wait for tomorrow."

He said the same on the next night. Only on the third night did we set out toward the border. Darkness covered us and, careful not to make a sound and be discovered, we progressed, step-by-step, toward the forest. We stopped after about two hours.

"We have reached the border," my guide said. "I cannot accompany you any further than this. I am fearful of the Germans and Russians. If you carry on straight," he pointed in the darkness to a general direction, "you will reach the town of Zaremby Koscielne. The Russians are there and from there you will be able to continue safely." He then disappeared into the darkness.

I had no choice. I was alone, trying to convince myself to believe the man's explanation. I began to walk. I walked for hours, an eternity. I feared death, having no idea whether I was walking straight or going around in circles. I cried, sang, talked to myself, and tried to stave off the fear. I walked, and walked, and walked.

At dawn, a thin light penetrated the tree tops. The distance between the trees slowly grew and I saw a church steeple from far off. I was extremely relieved that I had not miscalculated. Very soon I would arrive in the town. I quickened my steps.

"Go back!" I heard somebody shout in Russian and a soldier appeared out of nowhere, aiming his bayoneted rifle at me. I understood what he said, since Russian is similar to Polish, but I had absolutely no intention of going back. We slowly approached each other, he with his bayoneted rifle aimed at me, I with my increasing fear. How could I go back?

Then, glaring at me, discerning the fear in my eyes, the Russian soldier made a dismissive gesture that meant, "There is nothing I can do with this person." He sent me on my way, letting out an impressive Russian curse.

My knees shaking, my heart beating fast, I walked, following the train line that would lead me to the station. On reaching the station, I saw a train waiting for departure. It was brimming with people inside and trying to board it.

Relentlessly, I struggled with my body, pushing my way in, rocking forward, backward, and sideward with the sole aim of boarding that train. Fortunately, somebody in the toilet of the train opened a small window. With the urgency of a person struggling for survival, I unhesitatingly jumped up, held on to the window, and pulled myself up.

People standing below caught my legs and tried to pull me back down. The person inside the toilet pulled me back up. I wrestled and was pulled from above and below. I kicked those who were holding me back and was pulled by those trying to assist. In the end I succeeded, largely due to my small and thin frame.

At last, I was inside the train, riding with the others. Most of the passengers appeared to be Jewish evacuees for whom the Russian authorities had sent a train to take them inland.

After a short journey, the train stopped and we were ordered to disembark. We arrived at a huge displaced persons' camp called Ogrodniczki. There were tents for thousands of people and first aid stations, a true model of organization and order. All arrivals were registered and given food coupons. I was assigned a place in the bachelors' tent.

It was not long before we became instilled with a common aim, to return home. But how could we do that? Any plans we made fell through since we knew that the situation was grave. The Russian–German border was closed and any return route was blocked. We would have to wait.

When we were permitted to leave the displaced persons' camp, and free to come and go at will, we visited Bialystok, which was the closest city. We walked through its streets, searching for relatives or acquaintances among the masses of evacuees there. Like me, many tried to piece together bits of information about their families, to no avail.

We expected the Jews of Bialystok to come to our assistance, but they scorned us and regarded us as neglected and miserable evacuees. They avoided us to the extent of refusing us a glass of water to quench our thirst. Thus, isolated, alone, alienated, left to our own resources, and having nothing to do, we decided to sign up as candidates to work in the coal mines of Ural.

Toward the end of 1939, a Russian delegation arrived at

the camp to recruit laborers for the coal mines. My tent mates and I unanimously decided to apply for the work. When I realized that the minimum age was eighteen, and I was only seventeen years old, I changed my birth date by one year. When asked what my training was, I told them that I had been a radio technician in a factory.

After a two-week wait, I received a positive answer and soon found myself waiting with the others at the train station, ready to find a seat on one of the freight carriages that was already waiting at the station.

The wooden freight coaches became sleeping coaches, with a cast iron stove in their center, burning logs of wood, and a chimney to let the smoke out through one of the hatches on the side of the coach. There were bunk beds on both sides of the stove and fifty passengers in each coach, among them, a handful of women and families.

It was not long before the train whistle blew and we took our places on one side of the coach. We were on our way. Our destination was the Urals. It took us about a month to get there, with numerous stops on the way.

The view was enchanting, fascinating, and breathtaking. There were infinite expanses of dense forests on the one side and the *Taiga*[27] was on the other side. There were vast stretches of snow and a white wilderness of ice that seemed to reach the other side of the world. The sight was pure, clean, and blindingly immaculate. There was no sign of any settlement or human life. Here and there you could see a tree whose

27   Subarctic forest of evergreen trees.

branches and trunk had blackened, or a deer chasing after an animal, or being chased, leaving its tracks as a sign of life. The deeper we progressed into Russia, the heavier the snow fell from the heavens, concealing any tracks and covering the world with pristine new apparel. It was a splendid sight!

We purchased our food during the journey from a coach that had been converted into a canteen. We used the pocket money we received before boarding the train to buy sausages, cheese, and baked products.

The train occasionally stopped, allowing us to freshen up. The further we traveled into Russia, the more traffic there was on the railroad tracks. Coaches filled with people signified, more than anything else, the state of war in the world. Due to overcrowded railroad lines, our journey was sometimes delayed by several days by having to wait for another train to pass or waiting for another train to make way for our train. In such cases, we received a hot meal at the station, like everybody else. Sitting on chairs at long tables, we were served a hot meal and I especially remember the delicious, reddish, steamy fish soup, which we ate with great relish.

I had a terrifying experience at one of those stops. My companion and I went a way off from the train to relieve ourselves. When we heard the train whistle, we hurried back to the train just as everyone else did. However, we had ventured slightly too far away from the train and it started off without us. We ran and ran, trying to catch it.

Being a well-educated boy from Warsaw, I allowed my elders to get onto a train before me. The door and floor of the train were high and the train was starting to move. My friend and I were the last two to board. We knew that we had no hope of pushing ourselves back into the train. As a last resort, we both caught hold of the handle of the coach and found ourselves on the outer wall of the train. What a relief to at least be on the train!

For several moments, we were fascinated by the scenery whizzing past us, but then the freezing cold started to penetrate our bones and we jumped around on our two feet. We hugged ourselves, kept close to each other, and stuck to the side of the coach, hoping to elude the whipping wind as much as possible. We were frozen.

The train sped on, and by then we had already lost the feeling in our feet. We heard sounds of our friends trying to assist us from inside the coach. They were shouting, trying to encourage us and to stay in contact with us. They ran around, trying to find suitable tools to open up a way for us to enter by pulling out planks of wood. They and we were becoming desperate as we knew that time was running out and that there was nothing to be done. Time went on forever. At last the train stopped at a station.

Our friends quickly came out to us. We were by then as blocks of ice. They held us, carried us, placed us on the ground and covered us with snow. The snow massaged our bodies, stirring up the flow of blood. To this day I do not know how I survived that ordeal. I had been exposed to the freezing wind for an extended length of time at a temperature much below freezing point. I remained unscathed.

Our friends carried us into the coach, still massaging our bodies. Wrapped in blankets, we slowly thawed and only then did we dare to draw near to the heating stove. Our bodies warmed up and we were safe.

Nagornaia coal mine

Sverdlovsk Oblast, Kizel province, jurisdiction authority: Ural.

The province of Kizel was established in 1934. Important producing facilities were relocated there from the European part of Russia to safeguard them from the advancing Germans. The area was a highly developed industrial one due to large deposits of coal, iron, nickel, copper, gold, platinum, and other metals.

We disembarked the train, still dressed in our highly unsuitable urban clothing that had been hurriedly packed before our journey into the unknown. The freezing temperature of -20 degrees penetrated every cell of my body.

I remember standing in the area of the Nagornaia coal mine. Registration of our personal details was taking place in the office of a man named Krashevski, who was in charge of the district. I then found myself outside, on my way to the residential hut, my new home for the coming period of time. The freezing wind blew through the planks of the wooden hut, mocking the heating stove that tried unsuccessfully to warm the space.

I placed the mattress I had received on one of the beds and the few blankets on top. There were about twenty of us in that hut, and lacking sufficient blankets, we all lay down to sleep. We made a decision in the middle of the night. We would sleep together in pairs and keep warm with double the number of blankets covering us. We chose our partners carefully and resourcefully piled the blankets and the spare mattresses above us, wrapped ourselves up, and somehow managed to sleep through the night. We spent the first couple of nights in this way, until we settled in and received several more blankets.

When dawn broke on our first morning, we were greeted by the *politruk*, the political commissar. He was a Yiddish-speaking Jew who explained the daily routine and led us to the dining room for breakfast, for which we had to pay—as we did for all our meals.

Our hunger sated, we made our way to the office of Krashevski for a personal interview. When my turn arrived, I stood before him. He was leafing through the documents in front of him, then glanced at me, and shook his head as though in disbelief. He looked again at his papers, hesitated, and then asked, "Are you really from Radio Technik?"

"Yes," I replied confidently.

He stroked the nape of his neck, arranging the collar of his shirt. He looked at me once again, wrote something down, and included me in his list of mine workers.

The laborers were divided into three groups: coal miners, woodcutters for lining the walls of the mines and for laying the walking paths on the sinking snow, and service workers, such as tailors and shoemakers.

Still wearing our house clothes in which we had left Warsaw, we descended the mine. We returned at night, pitch-black and shivering with cold after the first day's work. We decided to declare a strike until we were provided with suitable clothing.

We were determined to start our strike the following morning. On hearing about this plan, the *politruk* insulted us by saying, "*Kinderlach*, children, are you aware of what you are doing? You are striking against your own interests. By refusing to work, you are harming the country's coal mine, your coal mine, and therefore you are harming yourselves."

We held negotiations; we voiced our opinion and he voiced his. We finally reached a compromise in which we elicited a promise from him. Whoever could do so, would descend the mine in his own clothing and the following day we would all be given work clothes suitable to the weather conditions. We agreed to these terms. Each of us received warm clothes, a coat and trousers lined with woolen material, a fur hat with ear flaps and shoes.

The misty mornings found us on a wooden planked path leading to the mine. Walking on the planks was difficult. We gingerly took it step-by-step, slipping, stumbling, trying to keep our balance, and hugging ourselves in an attempt to remain warm.

We were finally inside the mine, a new one that yet required work on its infrastructure. Wooden ladders divided into three-meter sections were built into the sides of the mine. Lanterns were hanging there to light the way into the depths of the mine.

We began our descent, rung by rung, slowly, cautious not to stumble or fall. Despite the gloves that were meant to keep our hands warm, holding on to the ladder was difficult owing to the ice that formed on the rungs of the ladder. Once I had managed to descend one section of the ladder, I continued to the next one. The deeper I went, the warmer it became as I gradually descended 100 meters underground.

My fellow workers and I changed into work clothes, consisting of a shirt and trousers made of coarse fabric, and shoes. Deep inside the belly of the earth, I joined a group of workers as an apprentice. My job was to widen the paths that had been dug out, to remove the coal stones by means of a pickax, to pile them up on the wagon and when it was full, to push it to an elevator together with another person. Then we would load the elevator, ring the bell, and wait for the person above to lift the load.

At the end of the work day, we once again climbed the ladders to the top. I was goaded to climb those difficult and frightening ladders by the urgency of departing from the mine, being outside, breathing fresh air, bathing, eating a warm meal, and resting.

And so, for three months, we worked day after day from morning to night, with only a short break for food and rest. Owing to this difficult physical work, all we wished for was some rest, only a little rest.

One day, I was called to the office of the chief engineer. "Tell me," Krashevski said, sizing me up. "Are you really from Radio Technik?" There was a reason for his surprise, since the Russian translation for "Radio Technik" is "radio technician who has graduated from the institute of technology." I was merely a thin young man. I replied in the affirmative, since I had worked at a factory called Radio Trio in Warsaw.

Krashevski still hesitated. Although he was not really inclined to believe me, he said, "Come with me," and led me out of the room to his office.

There were several outdated radios on the table. "Are you able to assemble one radio that works out of all these instruments?" I did not lose face, even though I had only worked as a messenger boy, taking components from worker to worker.

I gravely answered, "Look, Comrade Krashevski, each of these radio devices was manufactured in a different factory and their components are only compatible with those from the same factory. It is impossible to assemble a radio using parts from different factories." My reply seemed reliable enough to satisfy him.

"Come," he said and led me to the telephone exchange. I was introduced to Tshuvashov, a Chechen, who was in charge of the department. "This department is in need of somebody who can solve problems and failures in the equipment and in the communication lines. You, having technical knowledge, will be trained by Comrade Tshuvashov."

I was the happiest person in the world! That was the end of the coal mine for me.

The telephone exchange was extremely active since it served two mines operating in that area of the Urals. I received training, which included the task of climbing telephone poles on the road leading to the nearest town. The mine itself was one of the most important and sensitive spots for regular telephone communication, which was often a matter of life and death. This is how I found myself once again descending into the belly of the mine, this time as a telephone technician.

Despite the large amount of work and the minimal equipment, I enjoyed my work and felt fortunate.

One of the telephone lines collapsed during one of the most difficult storms, when snow was already piling up high and a cold wind was whipping the air. Communication with the regional center was lost and I was instructed to go out to inspect and repair the failure. Dressed in warm clothes with snow skis on my feet, I went out into the dark where the snow was swampy and the cold penetrated my bones

The telephone poles were planted along a division line in the forest, as protection against fires. The forest was thick, mysterious, and secretive. The raging storm created a misty scene and the silence around me was frightening. Everything looked white on a black background with a leafy branch jutting out here and there. In a different context, I would have stood in awe of this scenery, but not under those circumstances.

I advanced alone along the path, which extended for about 20 kilometers. I gradually progressed along the path, inspecting pole by pole, point by point. I was aware of the huge responsibility that I bore and inspected any possible cause of the problem. I eventually found the source. It was a disconnected wire.

I made my way up the utility pole, ledge by ledge. My hands and feet were quite frozen. There I was, repairing the telephone cable at the top of the pole, a difficult task at the best of times. After checking and verifying everything, I succeeded in restoring the communication line. Satisfied that all was well, I descended the pole in darkness. Reassured by the lights of the city in the distance, I made my way back in the direction of the railway station.

It was comforting to return to the mine and to the warm relaxation of a sauna bath. The sauna was our reward at the end of an exhausting day's work. It was built of wood and its steam blurred our vision. This was where we could console our tired bodies on the wooden benches lining the sides. Needless to say, I slept very well that night.

Our lives had a regular schedule. We worked five consecutive days and rested on the sixth. Soviet, communist, atheist Russia made its own rules regarding the day of rest. There was no seven-day week with a day of rest on the seventh day. There were no more Sundays, or Fridays. The day of rest was on a different day each week.

On the day of rest, we cleaned and tidied up the hut according to a duty roster. We laundered whatever clothing had not been sent to the laundresses for payment. We enjoyed eating our warm meals together, relaxing, and making plans for our future lives after we finished working at the mine. We dreamed about returning to our homes and families, about whom we knew nothing at all.

I began working at the coal mine in January 1940, in the heart of winter. Temperatures dropped to -30 degrees, and there was barely any daylight. Nature was generating strong snow storms and harsh winds.

Spring appeared suddenly, with a spurt. The sky became light blue and the sun shone. The blossoming trees were an unbelievably beautiful sight. A meadow of wild flowers of various colors sprung up all over the ground. There were reds and yellows, oranges, and purples, tall flowers and short ones, bundles of flowers and individual ones. Bushes awoke from their winter's sleep and the trees, garbed in green foliage, adorned themselves with their new garments.

The sight was magnificent. It seemed as though nature was announcing, "This is my gift to you after the onerous winter you have endured." When spring made way for summer, the long days united with the white, bright nights as though in compensation for the short, dark winter days. The world around was unbelievably beautiful.

Then the summer came to an end and made way for the fall. Again, the skies became gray, the days shorter, the first snow fell, and winter was once again the master of the region.

In September 1941, our contracts with the mine were about to expire. To our surprise, we were confronted with a refusal to release us from the contract, based on a lack of manpower. We protested and appealed to the workers' union. After a two-month delay, based on a decision of the workers' union, we were discharged and free to leave.

My friends and I packed our meager belongings. My earnings from the coal mine safely concealed in my knapsack, we bade a moving farewell to all those who had been part of our lives during that year, including Tshuvashov and the telephone exchange staff.

We boarded the south-bound train. I was only eighteen years old, but my childhood in Warsaw seemed very distant. It was during that time that I had read a book entitled *Tashkent,*

City of Bread,[28] which contained abundant descriptions of a place whose weather was warm and moderate and where bread was plentiful. Based on that story, Tashkent became our destination.

---

28   Written by Alexander Sergeyevich Neverov. The Hebrew translation by Avraham Shlonsky was published in 1932.

CHAPTER 5:
City of Tashkent, Uzbekistan

"Adults live in the outer realm of children's lives as children live in the outer realm of adults' lives.

"When will the joyful time come that children and adults will exist in parallel paths?"

- Janusz Korczak

Trains were the only form of transport in that region at that time, resulting in heavy railway traffic and limited train tickets. The journey took about a month since it consisted of many stops along the way. We were frequently obliged to change trains or wait at various stations until the arrival of a train that had vacant seats.

The seven of us divided into two groups wherever we were. One group usually stayed to guard our belongings, while the other purchased train tickets for the rest of the journey and went out to find food, which we bought at the local markets.

Despite the discomforts of the journey, I was awestruck by the beauty of the passing scenery. Traveling from the north toward the south-east, I felt as though I was emerging from darkness into the light, from the cold country into warmer areas.

We traversed the Taiga plains to the mountains and cliffs, blue lakes, and angry rivers. We traveled through desert plains colored with hues of red and black. The gray colors now became the gold and greens of the wild fields in the cultivated areas in which cotton was grown. In the cities, there were blue turrets of the domes, blending with the color of the skies.

The warmth encompassing the world intermingled with the glimmering feeling of spring in our hearts. We gradually peeled off items of clothing, feeling like birds that had been set free. Our journey eventually ended, marking yet another stage in our path of survival. We had reached Tashkent.

When we disembarked, we found ourselves at a train station awash with people. The Asiatic people were completely different from us in their dress and customs. We searched for a corner in which to settle down for a while, realizing that this would be our home for several days. As was our custom, we formed two groups; one to guard our belongings and the place we had appropriated for ourselves, and the other to scout the area and find something to eat.

Our first introduction to the city reminded me of what I had read in the book. Tashkent, whose name means "City of Stone," was characterized by an oriental appearance. The domes of its building were shades of turquoise; there were arches, Uzbek decorations, vine arbors on the rooftops, sheep wandering about, making their way through the masses of people, and roosters crowing their wake-up call. Tashkent of the book *City of Bread* kept its promise. There we tasted *lepyoshka*, Uzbek pitas, sweet rolls that I tasted for the first time, and *piroshki*, small puff pastries made of yeast dough and filled with delicious fillings.

After settling down, we sat down for a conference to discuss how we would support ourselves and find dwellings. We once again divided into two groups, one to guard and one to scout around the streets. The closer we approached the center of town, the more modern and western it looked. The city's streets were wide, bearing names of Russian leaders such as Stalin and Lenin.

One day, just as we were wandering around and speaking Yiddish, an obviously Jewish looking man walked by us and stopped. He had apparently been following us for quite a way, listening to our chatter in Yiddish and wondering who we were.

"*Kinderlach*, children, where are you from?" he asked.

We told him.

"Where are you lodging?"

"At the train station," we replied.

"Look, I am going to synagogue for the *aravit*[29] prayer. Come with me. We will pray and then we will ask the other people for advice about how to help you." We joined the man and went to pray at the synagogue, which was located in a

---

29   The evening prayer

secluded place. Each of us took a *siddur*[30] and a *kippah*[31] at the entrance. We prayed with several tens of other men.

"Jews," our benefactor addressed the congregation, "these young men who have joined us today are displaced and destitute people from Poland. They have an immediate need of lodgings. Anyone who is able must host one of them in his home. I am taking these two under my wing," he said, pointing to me and to my friend Zeev Gurfinkel, whom I had befriended in Ogrodniczki.

Each one of the seven of us soon had a host. Together with Zeev, I accompanied our host to his home. After consulting with his wife, they decided that I would stay at their daughter Sonia's home, which was located some distance away from the city center.

Sonia, who already had a child, was young and pretty. She came to fetch me from her parents' home and took me to her house, where she and her husband treated me as if I were part of their family. I was given a room for the next two weeks, at the end of which we thanked our hosts for their hospitality.

Zeev, another friend of ours, and I found out by chance that workers were needed at a factory that manufactured agricultural machinery in the city. The factory, which operated around the clock, was undergoing extension and construction. We reached the factory, asked for employment, and were hired as iron benders.

We found more than employment. There were living

---

30   A prayer book
31   A skullcap

quarters on the factory site, rented out to employees for a small sum. After registering, we were granted residence there, sharing one room between three of us. The bathroom and toilets were communal for all the residents. We would occasionally bathe at the public municipal baths.

Work at the factory was rigorous. We were obliged to bend the iron manually since there were no machines for this purpose. One of us would hold the rod using a long chisel, while the other would strike it with a 5-kilo hammer.

After several months, I received my first call up to the Russian army. One would wonder what connection a Polish citizen had to the Russian army. On my release from the coal mine in the Urals, I was issued with an identification card defining me as a Polish evacuee. The card granted me the rights of a temporary citizen while barring me from living in the main cities. I was, however, eligible for military service.

The Red Army

I was sent to a pre-military cavalry course. Since I was still considered a civilian, I continued working at the factory and living with my friends. Zeev, in the meantime, enlisted in the infantry.

I was entrusted with a black horse, of which I was, at first, afraid of approaching since I did not know him or his nature. Later, I remembered my grandfather's horses and the way he took care of them. I slowly learned how to come near to the horse, touch and stroke his head, or pamper him by giving him salt and sugar. We gradually grew close and the horse became familiar with my instructions through my body movements.

I was, of course, in charge of the horse's stable as well. I washed and brushed the horse, checked his hooves, and pampered him by stroking or flattering him.

One day, during the strenuous and lengthy training sessions, we were called to appear mounted on the horses at the Tashkent circus. This occurred after the beginning of the German–Russian campaign and we rode through the streets of the city proudly sitting upright, singing the anthem "We are fully prepared and loyal to go to battle for Stalin and the motherland ..." to the cheers of the crowds that had gathered to watch the parade. We performed a scene in the circus in which spies crossed the border and the cavalry, galloping on their horses, sent the spies away.

I warmly remember my days with the horses, which lasted until 7.22.1941. Although I worked among Russians, I felt I was one of them and not an outcast or a refugee. This was definitely a beautiful period that had a good effect upon me. Then the order arrived: The cavalry was to be dismantled and its men trained as drivers. The Russian leadership realized that the cavalry was outdated, owing to its heavy losses against the German artillery fire.

The driving course lasted six months, at the end of which I qualified as a truck driver and mechanic. The truck was nicknamed *Polotraka* ("A Ton and a Half"). During the course of my pre-military training as a horseman and driver, I was still considered a civilian and continued working at the factory, which was directly connected to the railway line that transported damaged tanks for repairs. At the beginning of the war, the factory moved to military production lines. Instead of agricultural machinery, it manufactured tanks and ammunition. I was confined to the place as an essential employee. Once I had a license, I requested to be stationed as a truck driver. Indeed I was given a car—a cabin that was attached to a trailer carrying bombs that I transported from place to place within the confines of the factory.

Life was arduous. Work was grueling, lasting twelve hours a day and my belly often remained hungry due to the lack of provisions.

1942

Nineteen Years Old

After working as a driver for several months, I was called up for army service. The former commander of the Polish cavalry, General Anders, organized a Polish armed force in Russia. Anders had been taken prisoner by the Russians and released after the Sikorski-Mayski Agreement. Anders' army consisted of Polish evacuees, people who had been released from labor camps, discharged officers, and Polish citizens who had previously served in the Russian army.

I was stationed as a driver in the unit located in Yangiyul, 30 kilometers from Tashkent. I became a soldier and was entrusted with a Russian jeep, an imitation of an American one. However, this role did not last very long. Anti-Semitism, apparently, has no bounds, and Polish hatred of the Jews found expression in the military as well, whether through accusations of "disloyal behavior," rivalry over roles, or simply out of pure hatred.

My commanders resented the fact that I, Itzchak, or Ignaz as they called me, was always sociable and friendly to everyone. Dissatisfied with me, they sent me back to the town major in Tashkent and to my former job in the factory. I also returned to my prior living quarters, sharing the room with Zeev and Leon.

This time, I found Tashkent, the City of Bread, starving for want of bread. The authorities began rationing food from the beginning of the war. Residents of Tashkent received two coupons—a bread coupon for daily use and a provisions coupon, distributed on certain occasions. Anyone engaged in manual labor was entitled to one portion of bread weighing 800 grams. White collar workers and women received 600 grams, while children received 400 grams of bread.

Government stations were set up for distributing the bread and the queues leading to these stations were obviously very lengthy. Bread coupons were valid for one month. At the beginning of every month, we were required to produce the old coupon in return for a new one.

Starvation was rife. We took advantage of any opportunity we had to buy bread for several days in advance instead of only for that day. Our stomachs defied any sort of reasoning. Once we had devoured the small portion of bread, we were left hungry for the other days. We would conclude our meals of bread with a cup of tea prepared from industrial substitutes. Instead of sugar, we used jam. We would pour the boiling water from a very large urn that was stationed in one of the rooms of the building in which we resided.

Every month, I purchased lunch coupons that entitled me to eat in the factory's dining room. The meal usually consisted of a plate of thin soup. Anybody who managed to scavenge food from other sources sold their coupons. I once bought such coupons and ate two or three portions for several days in a row.

Like the other starving people, my friends and I sought food on the black market. I do not know where these products originated, but large amounts of money could buy anything one wished to eat. Since we were unable to buy vegetables due to their high price, we settled for the prevalent food in those days of distress. This was cotton waste containing fibers and giving one a feeling of satiation. It was normally used as a food supplement for cows. The dough that was pumped out of huge containers was sold in different levels of hardness, from the softest to the toughest, which was impossible to chew. Having very little money, we had to be grateful for the toughest form of cotton waste.

Owing to problems caused by the deficient supply of electrical power, we were in need of kerosene, mainly for light and heat. Fortunately, I was a truck driver. Every day, I pumped out a very small amount of gasoline from the gas tank of the truck, cautious not to take too much. Since gasoline was distributed using a measuring tube in exchange for coupons, I would have been in huge trouble had I been caught stealing the gasoline from the tank. Thus, we used gasoline instead of kerosene. Zeev and I sold the leftover gasoline on the black market, using the money we earned to buy an additional piece of bread or another item.

We had another small source of income through taking passengers in the truck. I was sometimes required to make trips out of the factory and the city. There were always many people waiting at the passenger stations along the way. Although they were eager to get a ride, I was, in my capacity as a truck driver, forbidden to give people rides. However, I took these chances as I was afflicted by hunger, cold, and an empty pocket.

On my guard not to be caught by the police who were extremely strict, I occasionally offered rides to about twenty people at a time, for about 20 rubles each. They sat huddled up on the platform of the trailer, just as pleased about the arrangement as I was.

I remember one incident that still amuses me to this day. I once went out with Zeev to the black- market square. There was a fine assortment of communities and countries— Uzbeks, Russians, and Poles, all buying and selling their wares. We purchased a half a loaf of rough, black, whole meal bread with the money we earned from the gasoline that we sold. While we were negotiating our merchandise, an old man with a mandolin walked by. He plucked a few strings to try and persuade us that it was in order and that we should purchase it.

For some unknown reason, I found myself asking the man, "How much do you want for the mandolin?"

"Half a loaf of bread," he replied.

Without thinking twice, I handed the bread to him.

"What is happening here?" I heard Zeev shouting in anger. "Have you lost your mind? What do you think you are doing? Are you going to eat a mandolin?" He grabbed the bread and sent away the old man and the mandolin. This is how, for a fraction of a second, I pushed aside all reality amid all the chaos and distress that swept before us, a reality we could not escape.

The winter of 1943 was extremely difficult, not only regarding the weather, but on the military front as well. That winter, my friend Leon's bread coupon was stolen. There was no bread without a coupon, leaving him with absolutely nothing to eat.

Zeev and I tried to help Leon by sharing whatever food we had. Proud and independent, Leon often refused our offers. He starved for many days. His hunger-stricken belly started to swell, finally becoming ill with pellagra and requiring hospitalization. We hoped his condition would improve through medication and proper nutrition. We visited him as often as possible, trying to assist him, and hoping for an improvement. However, his strength failed him, and after several weeks in hospital, Leon passed away.

Zeev and I were asked to bring Leon to burial. How would we do this? Where would we take him? We stole gasoline and after several days, through deceit and distraction, we drove my truck through the gates of the factory, where every vehicle leaving or entering was strictly inspected. What would happen if anybody noticed our absence?

We were fortunate. When we reached the hospital, we

loaded our friend's coffin onto the truck and headed for the Jewish cemetery on the outskirts of the city.

"What do you want?" asked the guard at the gate of the cemetery.

"We wish to have a Jewish burial for our friend who has died," we replied.

"Do you have a death certificate?" We answered that we did not have one.

"Without a death certificate, we cannot perform the burial."

We were helpless and at a loss. Having no choice, we loaded the coffin back onto the truck and began to leave the place. As we turned to go, we noticed a row of empty burial pits. Looking around to make sure we were not being watched, we buried the coffin in one of the pits, covering Leon with clumps of earth as fast as possible. We saw the cemetery staff approaching us and quickly set off, without leaving any sign of identification on the grave.

We returned to the graveside several days later, flanking and creeping so as not to be seen. We found nothing that would serve as a sign of identification and commemoration. The mortality rate was so high in Tashkent that all the empty pits had already been filled by then with people whose strength ran out.

Heavyhearted, mourning, and cautious not to be noticed, we parted from Leon Bruckler of Warsaw, twenty-one years old, in his final repose. Zeev and I were haunted with feelings of remorse and regret for a long time after that. This time, I was reprimanded for leaving work.

Itzchak on his return to Warsaw, 1946

CHAPTER 6:

Return to Warsaw

"Evil walks about openly, while good waits for us to find it. Evil becomes public knowledge and demands an immediate response. Good hides from publicity and does not attract attention. By publicizing good, we prevent evil overcoming the good!"

- Janusz Korczak

1944

Dawn of a New Year

The coming year saw an improvement on the difficult period I had spent in Tashkent, in which life was a constant struggle for survival. The Russians had defeated the Germans in Stalingrad, and aided by America, they invaded Poland. The end of the war was in sight.

We, the Polish evacuees, heard word of a group being

formed by Wanda Wasilewska.[32] The aim of the organization was to enable us to return us to Poland. Anybody who wished to return home was requested to register. Once again, we were hopeful about our chances of returning home. We signed up, waited, and hoped.

5.8.1945

I do not recall whether the sun's rays caressed the world on that morning, or whether clouds covered the skies. At any rate, for us the sun was shining. On waking that morning, ready for work, we were surprised to see a mass of people running to and fro, shouting out one word: "Vic-to-ry." The Germans had surrendered. There would be no more horrors of war.

Who would have believed this day would arrive?

Zeev and I ran to the factory as an arrow that is fired from a bow, like birds that have been set free from their cage. Everyone present was intoxicated with victory and alcohol, congratulating and hugging each other, not engaging in any kind of work. When the German surrender was signed at nine

32   Polish author and communist political activist who played an important role in the reestablishment of the Polish army during World War 2 and the formation of the People's Republic of Poland.

o'clock, we were already all drunk with wine, cheering and celebrating that day of victory.

The very next day, we started organizing our journey back to Warsaw. We contacted the Polish army so that they could prepare the necessary papers for us. Once we had the documents, we had several months' wait until our turn arrived to return to Poland, after the discharged soldiers had first been sent back home. On a spring day in 1946, we were called up to report to the train station. Once again, we were aboard a train awash with people under dreadful conditions. Our journey lasted about one month.

During all those days on the train traveling toward Poland, leaving the Russian plains in which traces of the war were evident, I was filled with thoughts about why I was actually returning. I wondered what and whom I would find on my return. After all, I had completely lost contact with everyone after I had left Poland, and had obtained no information about them at all.

We crossed the Polish border. The closer we came to our destination, the more horrible the sights were. We saw destroyed villages, skeletons of burned trees, and scorched, destroyed land. We saw vast stretches void of any signs of life. A strange silence enveloped us and we had the sensation of having reached an unfamiliar place.

In another moment the train would enter the train station. The pressure in my chest was rising. Warsaw East was the final stop. I so much wanted to go home. But there was no home to return to.

Is this Warsaw?

This is the question we asked ourselves, shocked and silent. Numbness and amazement replaced our excited expectations of returning home. This was most certainly not the same Warsaw I had left six years previously.

The city was destroyed and crushed. Its buildings were stone ruins, its streets and roads were mounds of rubble. Nothing remained of the glory of its past. The very air carried tidings of tragedy and death.

Shadows of people moved around the ruins of the ghetto. These were displaced persons from the labor and concentration camps, desperately searching for a sign of the homes they had left, or a relic of their families.

There had been a building at the end of Krochmalna Street. This was my aunt and uncle's house, the house in which my family lived until I departed from them all—my grandmother and grandfather, mother, brothers and their families, and my sisters. Nothing remained. There was no house, no family.

I walked around the area of the ghetto with Zeev, always with Zeev, giving each other strength. A deathly silence enveloped the place that had in the not too distant past been populated by so many Jews. Where were they all? Where were my grandfather, grandmother, mother, my brothers and sisters? And where had all those Jews, about a half a million of them, vanished to? Had they been murdered and erased from the earth?

The warm, bright glow of summer was in sharp contrast to the empty, ruined, and blackened buildings. It seemed as though the broken walls of each house were narrating a perpetual story. Here and there, we could see workers or residents attempting to clear out the wreckage. Were they trying to sweep away what had happened here, to conceal it?

We walked through the memories feeling distressed, failing to understand or internalize the sights we saw. It all seemed like a delusion. Is this what hell looks like? What were those sounds that I heard? Was it my imagination or did I hear the sound of the crowds on the throbbing and thriving Jewish street? Were the voices from the past interwoven with the shouts of disaster on discovering the horrible reality? Who were those figures walking before my eyes? Could they be my friends from the past? Was I hallucinating? The images became shadows walking away from me, disappearing from view into nothingness.

Having already taken possession of the wreckage, the Poles regarded us as enemies trespassing on their property. They feared that we would claim our belongings, which had been forcibly stolen from us through plundering and hatred. They were driven by anti-Semitism. Always in groups for fear of being attacked if appearing alone, the displaced persons gathered together in an odyssey of return to a remnant of the past.

I wished to return to my grandfather's home, but I was unable to do so as I lost my way in the labyrinth of ruins blocking every plot of land. I lost hope. Bands of Poles provoked and conspired against the Jews, thwarting their attempts to approach the buildings. I returned to Krochmalna Street in an attempt to catch a glimpse of number 92, the orphanage, which had been my home. From a distance, I saw that a bomb had hit the magnificent attic, destroying it and leaving no trace of Dr. Korczak's room. The rest of the building was intact. I approached the entrance, hoping to enter it, to cling to memories of the past. I heard the voices of children from the courtyard. These were Polish children. The orphanage had become a boarding school for gentile children. It seemed to me that my home had been stolen from me. I took flight.

My body shivered on the first evening of my return to Warsaw, not from cold, but from the visions of that day and the flashes of understanding that shook me. I was alone in the world, the sole survivor of my entire family. I craved the company of others and the sensation of the throbbing of life. I headed toward the Jewish Center.

The Joint[33] and UNRWA[34] had opened information and assistance centers in Warsaw. This was our first destination as we disembarked from the train in Warsaw. We supplied our personal details and identification documents, and were duly registered. We hoped that this information would serve as records for our relatives and friends whom we hoped were looking for us too. We also expected to be able to find our dear ones who perhaps had also registered at the center. The center granted us any assistance they could, but there was not a trace or sign of the fate of my or Zeev's families. The stark reality of "never again" seemed like a slap in our faces.

---

33   American Jewish Joint Distribution Committee

34   United Nations Relief and Works Agency

Encounters with displaced persons of the camps at the center painted a grim picture of the horror and the extent of the tragedy that had befallen the Jewish people, including families of people like mine. Our sense of reason failed to comprehend our loss. Our emotions could not contain the stories of hatred, cruelty, abuse, and annihilation our people had suffered.

While I heard the tales interrupted by sobs of pain and loss, I saw images of the past, images of a magnificent Jewish community living in this place until only very recently. There had been hundreds of thousands of people, families with their children living their lives and participating in culture, religion, education, and study, and intellectuals who had an impact on the entire Jewish world. Where were the Orthodox Jews, and Jews that spoke only Yiddish in their everyday lives? Where was the secular population that enriched Poland through its contributions to cultural life? Where had all this gone? How could this horror, for which we did not even find a word, have occurred in such an enlightened society?

A word was cast into the air, bringing my thoughts back to reality. This word was to accompany our Jewish lives forever. The word was *Holocaust*.

The house on Krochmalna Street

Zeev and I returned to the ruins of the ghetto the following day. We searched the wreckage once again, as if we were possessed. Perhaps we had overlooked something. Perhaps we would find a memory or a relic. But there was no such thing. All that was left was a small part of the ghetto wall that had survived as a monument to the overcrowded place that had housed so many Jews.

We returned to Krochmalna Street as well. This time, I entered the building. I went up the stairs leading to the large hall. The place looked quite different, even alien. There were no tables in the dining room, no piano, or playing area.

A woman approached me. I introduced myself as a former student.

"May I ask you a few questions about the building?"

She replied that she had no information and that the office was now closed.

"Please come back another time," she said.

The next time I dared to step inside the building was almost forty years later. In 1983, the Janusz Korczak Association held a reunion in the building for children of the orphanage. I participated, although I had a dreadful feeling. By then I knew what the fate of the doctor, Miss Stefa, and the children had been. The thought of a Christian boarding school operating on those premises was almost too horrible for me to bear. The Korczak Association made several unsuccessful attempts to obtain ownership of the property.

I clearly remember the first time I learned about the fate of Korczak, Miss Stefa, and the children. One evening, on returning to the Jewish Center in Warsaw, I plucked up the courage and asked a Polish clerk manning one of the offices.

"Excuse me," I said in Polish. "Could you please answer a few questions?" He agreed, and I asked him if he had any information about Dr. Janusz Korczak and the orphanage he managed. He immediately gave a decisive answer, "Sir, of course I know. People say that after they were exiled to the ghetto, they were sent somewhere." Distressed, I did not ask any further questions.

Zeev and I wandered around Warsaw. During the day, we searched for information and relics and by night we returned to the center. Being outdoors was dangerous for us. We were homeless and displaced people with no families. My feeling was that Poland had betrayed me and erased my past and that of my family and people.

We felt estranged and sensed the animosity of the Holocaust-denying Poles. We found ourselves despised amid people who suddenly seemed alien. The only time I ever heard a word of apology from a Pole was years later, during a visit to Treblinka. I told a group of people the story of my family's holocaust and the story of Dr. Korczak. After hearing my story, the Pole approached me and expressed his apology.

When Zeev and I realized that our hopes of finding anything—a sign or a memory among the rubble—would come to nothing, we moved to Lodz following word of a large Jewish organization for displaced persons that had opened up on St. Jacob Street. As in Warsaw, although we received full support regarding food and lodging, we found not one name uniting us with members of our families.

At a certain point, we were struck with the dreadful realization that we alone would have to bear their memory and would have to be responsible for telling the story of Jewish Warsaw, which had been wiped off the face of the earth. From then on, the following disturbing questions offered me no repose.

How could the world remain silent in the presence of these horrors that occurred in Poland? Did nobody protest or resist the construction of those camps on Polish soil? Was there any assistance during the Warsaw Ghetto uprising? After all, we were Polish citizens living in its capital city. There were no answers.

Through my oppressive feeling of loss, I realized that I wanted to—and ought to—leave Poland, the country that had become the largest cemetery of the Jewish people.

I internalized the events of the Holocaust. The visions became engraved in my heart, inscribed in my memory. These visions keep returning to me to this very day.

My Family

Top right: My brother Moshe's wife; to her left, my father Haim. Second row from top: My oldest brother Moshe and his baby daughter; my mother Esther; grandmother Henia; grandfather Yehezkel.

Third row from the top: My oldest sister Haya; my youngest brother Velvaleh (Zeev); my brother Alter and his wife and baby daughter.

Bottom row: My little sister Miriam

CHAPTER 7:

Commemorate and Create

"Any form of expression for remembering the Holocaust is positive and desirable. It is essential not to allow indifference and oblivion to reign."

- Itzchak Belfer

"Sculpture and painting on cloth have now come down to the galleries, no longer being found only on ceilings and walls of temples."

- Janusz Korczak

dr. A. Goldsmit
(J. Korczak)

1878-1942

J. Beffer

Elders of the City—Printing ink on paper 38 X 57

The Ghetto Children—Watercolor on paper 35 X 50

The Mother—Printing ink on paper 50 X 70

Portrait of Janusz Korczak—Oil on canvas 50 X 70

Despair—Printing ink on paper 35 X 50

The Escape—Printing ink on paper 35 X 50

Homeless—Printing ink on paper 35 X 50

Fear—Printing ink on paper 35 X 50

In Distress—Printing ink on paper 35 X 50

Ghetto in Flames—Printing ink on paper 60 X 80

CHAPTER 8:

Toward a New Life

"Usually, weak people are the ones who fight for justice and strong people fight for peace. People do not listen to each other. This is why a social code of laws is necessary."

- Janusz Korczak

*A*liyah[35] activists from Israel were present in Europe at that time, especially representatives of political parties who came to gather the survivors and train them for *aliyah*.

Zeev and I joined the organization *Nocham*,[36] which was similar to *Gordonia*[37]. Together with other youngsters, survivors, and displaced persons from the camps, we formed a group that planned to make *aliyah* to *Eretz Israel*. It was

---

35   Immigration to *Eretz Israel*

36   *No'ar Halutzi Me'uhad* (United Pioneer Youth)

37   Zionist youth movement

there that I was first introduced to *Eretz Israel* and the seed of yearning for our own homeland was planted in my breast.

Zionism was no longer merely a concept; it became tangible. I became aware that *Eretz Israel* is my true and only homeland. I then remembered Miss Stefa and Dr. Korczak's animated descriptions of the beautiful scenery they observed during their visits to *Eretz Israel*. They spoke enthusiastically of the wonderful pioneering spirit, the atmosphere of building, the *kibbutzim, moshavot*[38] and *moshavim*.[39] They spoke about overcoming challenges and the achievements of the pioneers.

We learned Hebrew in the *Nocham* youth movement and lived in a training kibbutz in which we managed our own lives. Our hearts were bursting with renewed hope for the future.

But encounters with other refugees and survivors of forced labor and concentration camps were distressful. Through stories told by the others, I learned about the years during which I was absent from Poland.

The members of the group painfully whispered their stories, unable to face their bleeding bodies and souls. They told horror stories of physical abuse, which had tainted their spirits. Not everyone spoke or told their story, although a few had the courage to relive the suffering. The horrible agony of which they spoke stabbed at my heart, since I could only imagine what my family had endured. I shudder from the depths of my heart when I think of them.

Since Polish hatred of the Jews was undisguised, we feared

---

38   Settlement, individually owned property

39   Settlement, a type of cooperative agricultural community

physical harm, and arranged guard duty in the buildings we inhabited.

Polish people had suffered and been persecuted by the Germans. It was, and still is, difficult to image that these same Polish people despised, hated, and harmed the Jews, instead of identifying with us and demonstrating humanity and mutual assistance to their brothers in suffering. We waited impatiently for our turn for *aliyah*, so we could leave hatred-filled Poland behind us.

Zeev and I went to Wroclaw through Nocham, joining a group of young people like ourselves from the *aliyah* organizations. In Wroclaw, we participated in a training workshop for leaders of *aliyah* groups, which sprung up every now and then. We studied Hebrew, geography of *Eretz Israel*, and Zionism. While in Wroclaw in 1946, approximately one year after the end of the war, we heard word of the cruel pogrom against the Jews of Kielce, in which Poles slaughtered forty-seven people and injured many others. Undoubtedly, the despicable Kielce pogrom reinforced my conviction that the only place for me was in *Eretz Israel*.

The youth leader seminar at Wroclaw—Itzchak is in the bottom row, third from the left.

Tidings of our *aliyah* to *Eretz Israel* arrived several months later, during the summer. We were notified as follows: "Be prepared. You will be leaving tomorrow. Your first destination is crossing the Polish-Czechoslovakian border." We each packed a bag and the following morning I found myself sitting beside Zeev on a tarpaulin–covered truck, en route to Czechoslovakia.

The journey through Czechoslovakia was swift. We continued on to Austria, stopping at a large displaced persons' camp that had been set up on the outskirts of the city of Steyr, in northeastern Austria. The camp housed thousands of refugees in buildings spread out according to political affiliation. We too had accommodation. We ate our meals in shifts in the communal dining room. The camp had a kosher kitchen.

We occupied ourselves with study and participation in cultural activities. We occasionally went out in small groups to walk around the streets of Steyr. The weather was warm and inviting, in contrast to the cool and aloof attitude of the Austrians toward us. We were made to feel as if we were merely specks of dust to be brushed from a garment, transparent and unworthy of any attention.

Months passed and the warm summer retreated, bringing fall winds. We moved again, this time to a displaced persons' camp at Salzburg. After several weeks, we continued on to Innsbruck, a distance of about 30 kilometers from the Alps, our last stop before crossing the border into Italy. This border crossing was considered convenient since it was the lowest crossing point between the two countries. We experienced the first few days of winter while we were in Innsbruck. On our departure, we felt the frost penetrating our bones.

Our journey was led by emissaries of the organization *Bricha*,[40] which had been founded by Abba Kovner. The aim of the organization was to assist Jewish Holocaust survivors, mainly from Poland, escape post-World War 2 Europe to the British Mandate for *Eretz Israel* in violation of the White Paper of 1939.

---

40   Escape or flight, in Hebrew

Itzchak and Zeev at Steyr

Women, children, and men, old and young people, attentive and animated, spent the first part of the journey crowded onto trucks. At the end of the truck ride, we continued by foot. We reached a certain point where we waited for someone to appear and guide us on the rest of the route, but to no avail. Fortunately, we waited only a few days. Crossing the alpine pass was a difficult feat, especially in the dark and the freezing cold weather. Boulders and tumbling rocks hampered our progress. Small children stumbled, clinging on to their weary mothers. The elderly gnashed their teeth but stubbornly persevered, step-by-step, in an endeavor to avoid becoming a burden or holding up the convoy.

We were overcome with fear of being caught crossing the border illegally and deported back to Poland. During those long hours of walking, climbing, and crawling, I once again had a formidable sense of being persecuted and unwanted, having no homeland. Indeed, all three countries bordering the alpine passes—Nazi Austria, Fascist Italy, and neutral Switzerland—refused to grant us recognition. None of them had any compassion for us, the weary and persecuted people.

In Italy

After walking, staggering, slipping, and crawling for so many hours, we finally crossed the border. The words, "You are now in Italy," sounded like a song of praise. At daybreak, tired as we were, we were elated to see the magnificent scenery, the beauty of the Italian villages clinging to the side of the mountains, coloring the world, it seemed, with magical colors from fairy tales. The rising sun restored hope in our hearts for a more promising future.

We were once again on the trucks, headed this time for 5 Via Union, Milan, which was the center for *aliyah* operations. After registration and rest in Milan, we continued on to Bologna where we were accommodated in a magnificent Italian villa, surrounded by dreamlike scenery.

With members of the group in Bologna (Itzchak is sitting second from left)

Still waiting for our turn to leave for *aliyah*, each one of us participated in daily chores. We continued to receive enrichment lessons in Hebrew and history. It was at this time that my artistic talents were revealed through scribbling on scraps of paper that I managed to obtain.

I was asked to decorate the walls of the hall that served as our meeting place for social activities and study. I, of course, agreed. I used watercolors on sheets of paper supplied by the emissaries from *Eretz Israel*, painting everything I could imagine, and especially focusing on portraits of the Zionists leaders of the time. I did not even know them but based my paintings on photographs I had seen in newspapers from *Eretz Israel*, still known as Palestine in 1946.

"Itzchak," I was asked one day by a visiting emissary, "would you agree to decorate other centers with your paintings as well?" I agreed without hesitation. This is how I found myself in Selvino, in the province of Bergamo, on a farm that had previously housed Fascist Italian youth and after the war became a refuge, providing food, shelter, and rehabilitation to hundreds of Jewish orphan survivors of the Holocaust.

The farm contained one large central building for general activities and residences. I, Itzchak Belfer, twenty-three years of age, and an orphan like the children, was asked to teach them to draw. This I did not manage to do.

In the period of organization before their studies began, I participated in a volleyball game. I was familiar with this game from home and was a fairly competent player. However, I fell and broke my ankle during a failed darting leap. I spent the next couple of days in the orthopedic ward of the Bergamo hospital with my leg in a plaster cast. I was then introduced to Chianti, Italy's most famous wine, which we often drank with our lunch. I was hospitalized for a long period of time, since I had a complex fracture.

There was a priest who visited hospital patients wishing to confess. One day, he came up to my bed and placed the cross he was holding close to my lips for me to kiss it.

"*Io Ebraico*," I said, already having learned several words of Italian. "I am a Jew."

"Never mind," he unhesitatingly replied. "You may confess nevertheless."

While still in hospital, I parted from my dear friend Zeev, who was among the fifty people who were flown to *Eretz Israel* in Operation Michaelberg, the only clandestine immigration by air from Italy.

When my ankle was strong enough, I returned to Selvino for a period of recuperation. However, I was not fit enough to participate in activities. I felt uncomfortable as I was unable to contribute to the work pool, feeling that I was a guest who had arrived there for a vacation. The managers of the facility told me not to worry about this, saying, "Your eligibility for *aliyah* has not been compromised and your place on the list is being kept."

The following days were spent in forced idleness, although I drank in more and more of the beauty and charm of Italy. My thirst remained unquenched.

I became lucky when one of the managers of the facility said to me one day, "Itzchak, in Ostia, a large neighborhood of Rome, we are operating a school for fishing and shipping.

The walls of the school need decorating. Would you mind moving there to contribute your artistic talents and decorate the place?" I soon found myself in Scuola a Pesca e Marineria, situated in the Lido di Roma, the ancient port of Rome. To my surprise, I discovered how much I loved the sea. This love has lasted to this day, and has also affected the rest of my family.

My first days in Ostia were spent painting, as promised. Portraits of Zionist leaders adorned the walls of the rooms. Inquisitive as usual, I snuck in to listen to lectures. Since they were in Italian, I managed to find a Romanian who translated the content of the lessons into our common language, Yiddish. The purpose of the course was to train approximately thirty young displaced persons to be involved in clandestine immigration to *Eretz Israel*.

Paolo, the fisherman, taught fishery. The *Capitano*, as we called him, taught shipping. I easily abandoned my artistic and cultural endeavors and joined the group of youngsters, leaving with them in their boat to ride the waves, to fish at night for the following day's lunch, to learn swimming, seamanship, and shipping. If my memory serves me correctly, there was not one occasion in which our boat did not capsize and fall into the water.

This was a period of immense happiness. I was young and I felt my youth. I enjoyed the company, the feeling of belonging, and I became addicted to life. At the end of each day of work and study, we went out into the streets, eyeing the beautiful girls who were walking about, enjoying the tenor voices of the street singers who were entertaining the passersby and the street players who gathered small crowds around them, and enjoying the Italian delicacies. Yes, I painted here and there. I drew the wide open sea, with all of its shades of blue.

9.15.1947

Eight years and two weeks had passed since that bitter moment that changed my life and dictated my destiny, since that rushed parting from my family and my home in those troubled times. I was standing on the deck of a clandestine immigration ship that would take me home over the waves, to *Eretz Israel*.[41] Earlier on, I had made the necessary preparations, the journey in the middle of the night on a rumbling truck to the port city of Genoa. Not far from the shore, with lights extinguished, she was waiting for us. Her name was *Af Al Pi Chen*.[42]

Af Al Pi Chen was the first ship to bring displaced persons to *Eretz Israel* after the *Exodus* affair. The *Exodus* was a clandestine immigration ship whose passengers were forcibly expelled from Haifa Port to British detention camps in Germany on 7.18.1947 after a bitter struggle.

The *Af Al Pi Chen* was the last of the clandestine immigration ships. Its passengers rebelled and actively opposed the British soldiers who tried to take control of the ship, in an attempt to prevent their arrest and expulsion to detention camps in Cyprus. The ship's name was given in defiance of the government of the British Mandate, especially the *Exodus* af-

---

41   The Land of Israel

42   The literal translation of the ship's name is "Despite It All."

fair, which forcibly prevented hundreds of displaced persons from debarking in *Eretz Israel*.

The ship was converted from a tank landing craft to an Italian cargo boat. It was then acquired by *Mossad Le'Aliyah Bet*[43] and equipped to serve as an immigration ship. Owing to the ship's ability to sail in shallow waters, the *Mossad* people planned to let off its 434 passengers, all Holocaust survivors, onto the beach. The ship's commander was Yitzhak Landauer, and the captain was an Italian.

We made our way to the ship in complete silence so as not to be revealed. A rope stretched between barrels showed us the way. There were thirty people in my group. Trained as seamen, we were assigned the role of sailors and remained on the deck. All of the others were taken down to the lower deck and instructed to remain there during the entire voyage. It was overcrowded and stifling, certainly no pleasure-cruise, but the passengers' desire and hope to reach *Eretz Israel* was powerful enough for them to overcome those uncomfortable conditions.

The ship sailed under an Italian flag. As we made progress, the flag was replaced according to the territory in which we sailed, whether it was Turkish or Greek. After a week of sailing, we approached the coast of Alexandria, Egypt. Sailing now under an Egyptian flag, we approached El Arish. Suddenly a low-flying airplane appeared, circled the ship several times, and then disappeared. We realized that we had been discovered. Since there had been nobody on the deck at that

---

43   Literally, "Institution for Immigration B."

moment, we hoped that the ship had not aroused suspicion and that it had been taken for a cargo ship on its way to unload its cargo at the harbor. We were wrong.

The ship increased its speed, but soon three British destroyers surrounding it. The British signaled us the direction in which to sail, and announced on a loudspeaker: "You must surrender. You are prisoners. The rest of the voyage will be made under our commands."

The Italian captain disappeared from sight. His place was taken by one of the emissaries from *Eretz Israel* who accompanied the voyage. He steered the ship in the direction of one of the destroyers and increased the speed, ramming into the destroyer with all its force and causing it damage.

The youngsters among us, who had gathered on the upper deck, all fell backward. The British soldiers did not give up. We watched them as they planned to enter the deck on which we were standing. Armed with clubs, shields, and helmets, they lined up in rows to jump or to hang onto ropes.

We, too, prepared ourselves. The deck became flooded with stones and hundreds of canned food goods of all shapes and sizes that had been brought up from the belly of the ship. This was our ammunition. Eventually, the British boarded the ship. They beat us with their clubs and we retaliated by throwing cans of food at them. A sharp blow to my back threw me to the ground. When I came to my senses, I got up and continued to fight.

We fought like lions, with all our force. Several illegal immigrants were wounded and required medical treatment. We resisted surrender for as long as our ammunition held out but finally our combat ceased. All the passengers that had been crowded into ship's belly were brought up to the deck, flogged by their captors. We were lined up in rows.

We could not believe our eyes. A young woman who had sailed with us from Genoa marched the British through the rows and in fluent English pointed out the emissaries from Israel, exposing them to the British. She was obviously a collaborator with the British, being the daughter of a woman who had married an officer of the British secret police. During the journey, we had seen her in the cockpit on several occasions, but we were aware of her sociability and did not suspect anything. She had been responsible for signaling the ship's exact location to the British, singling out the ship's crew, including the Italians, thereby exposing them to the British.

The illegal immigrants attempted to damage the ship after being ordered to disembark at Haifa Port. However, the British prevented this from occurring. At this point, several immigrants were wounded.

Once in Cyprus, we heard that a death sentence had been imposed on us. After the British seizure of the ship, we were forcibly taken to Haifa Port, ordered to disembark the ship, and then again forced onto the British destroyers, which served as floating prisons. The destroyers then made their way to the detention camps in Cyprus. We were now under lock and key.

Cyprus
Winter Refugee Camp 68.

Xylotymbou, a short distance north of Larnaca, Cyprus.

After being deported to Cyprus from Haifa aboard the destroyer, we were transported to Xylotymbou in closed trucks. There was another winter camp not far from us, at Dhekelia and the summer camp at Caraolos, near Famagusta. The difference between the summer and winter internment camps lay solely in their types of accommodation. The winter camp had tin huts occupied by about eighteen people, while the summer camp consisted of tents, each holding eight occupants. Besides this slight difference, the camps were identical in their format, which was that of low-budget British military bases.

Being at Xylotymbou was a traumatic experience for me. After feeling relatively liberated, I was once again deprived of my freedom, and my life was ruled by others. It was inconceivable then, as it still is today, how human beings, in this case the British, could treat the Holocaust survivors, after all that they had undergone during the war.

The Xylotymbou site consisted of five winter camps. Camp 64 was for administration and public activities. Camp 65 was assigned to children. Betar[44] members were in Camp 66 and

---

44   Betar is a Revisionist Zionist youth movement which was founded in 1923.

Hashomer Hatzair[45] members were in Camp 67. Camp 68 was a registration base. Two other camps, numbers 70 and 71, were later added at nearby Dhekelia.

The camp reminded us of the camps of suffering in Germany—barbed wire fences surrounding the camps, watchtowers, tanks patrolling around the camp, and constant, close control, as if it were a high security prison. All of these contributed to our depressed state of mind.

After registration at Camp 68, we received personal equipment, which consisted of a camp bed, a blanket, and a pillow. After a short transition period, a tin hut became my place of abode in Camp 67 during the whole of that period. My main concern was the uncertainty of my future. When it became apparent that the future was to be easier than we had expected, we started to organize our lives.

The British permitted the emissaries and selected people in the camp to lead us in self-management, in order to save themselves the bother of having to do so themselves.

Supported by the Joint,[46] school classes were held for children and adults. There was an infirmary, religious services, a clothing distribution station, and everything required for our day-to-day lives. We were allowed to wake up at any time we wished. The person on duty brought food from the communal kitchen for all of our meals, which we ate in the tin

---

45   *Hashomer Hatzair* (The Youth Guard) is a Socialist–Zionist, secular Jewish youth movement which was founded in 1913.

46   American Jewish Joint Distribution Committee

hut. Another person on duty was in charge of cleaning up after each meal. The days ended with a concert, lecture, performance, sing-along, or play, which quenched our thirst for culture. For the rest of the time, we were free to engage in any activity we wished.

Happily for us, the displaced persons included artists, painters, and sculptors, including Abba Fenichel and Herman Zvi. The leadership in *Eretz Israel* encouraged the study of art as a tool for dealing with the effects of the Holocaust, our uprooting, and expulsion. The British realized that the busier we were, the better it would be for them, and permitted artists to visit the camps for certain periods of time in order to give workshops. Among those artists were Naftali Bezem and the sculptor Zeev Ben-Zvi.

I joined these classes, since I was eager to study art. I especially loved to be in the presence of Zeev Ben-Zvi and to enrich my world through his teachings. The chance encounter with him was a most significant factor in my artistic career. Thanks to him I was infected with the "bug" for drawing and sculpture. This dear man, a pure artist, was good at penetrating my soul, allowing me to release the sketch artist in me. After all, a painter or sculptor should first know how to sketch well. There is no doubt in my mind that it was he who made me understand the essence of sculpture, to apply an idea to a three-dimensional creation.

I loved to touch and feel the raw material, to understand its creative capabilities. I devoted myself to the discovery of sculpture, since clay was readily available and there was a steady supply of plaster.

At this point, I was appointed to be the painter of the winter camps, a position for which I was paid two pounds sterling each month. Nobody was happier than me. Once again, portraits of Jewish and Israeli leaders, authors, and artists adorned the walls of the huts. I converted the unused huts into cultural rooms, bringing furniture from wherever I could and placing books and newspapers on the tables, thereby creating corners for socializing and rest.

Our physical exercise took the form of football. Each camp had its own team and league games were routine.

In between all of these activities, there was full cooperation between the *Haganah*[47] and the camps' administration to train us for pre-military service. This was, of course, carried out clandestinely in one of the tents, without the knowledge of the British. Training was compulsory for the children and was carried out in a military fashion. At the end of each phase, we were promoted to a higher rank. We were obliged to report at every command. Our training included learning how to dismantle, clean, and assemble Sten and Czech rifles that were smuggled into the camp, hidden from the watchful eyes of the guards.

Our training took place in an area we called the *Negev*, a desolate region between camps 67 and 70. We dug tunnels at night, despite the brightness of the floodlights. We carried the soil out of the tunnels in our pockets and later threw it into the lavatory huts, blocking the sewage pits, to the bewilderment

---

47   Jewish paramilitary organization in the British Mandate
        from 1920 to 1948.

of the British. When this happened, Greek workers employed as servicemen by the British were called in to dig and connect new pits.

One of these Greek workers became acquainted with one of the people living in my quarters, also of Greek origin. The worker would supply his friend with olives, who was delighted, and ate one olive after another. I watched my friend devouring the olives with great interest. Being of European origin, olives were a novelty for me. I tasted one and spat it out, not being accustomed to its bitter taste. Since arriving in Israel I have since learned to enjoy eating olives.

News was broadcast over the loudspeaker in the camps. The interpretation of the news was varied in each camp, according to the political party to which it was affiliated. We, members of *Hashomer Hatzair*, were angered by what sounded like a distortion of facts and propaganda coming from the *Betar* camp. We demanded that they change the nature of their broadcasts and even set an ultimatum of twenty-four hours, otherwise….

We armed ourselves with sticks, which were intended to persuade the opposite side to adopt our point of view. We surrounded the loudspeaker at the center of their camp. Eventually, we did not use our sticks. The problem was resolved through negotiation.

The image described above is an example of normal daily life. However, we were incarcerated in the camps surrounded by barbed wire. Deep inside, we longed for a life of freedom.

11.29.1947
in Cyprus

The UN General Assembly voted to partition Palestine into two states, one Jewish and the other Arab (the Partition Plan), on 11.29.1947. Our joy was boundless at the news of the vote, which was broadcast over the camp loudspeakers. Feeling that our release from incarceration in the detention camp was drawing near, we dressed in our best clothing as if for a festival lasting several days.

I remember the tension between the British and ourselves prior to that day, each side for its own reasons. We gained courage from the hope that at last we would have our own country and freedom and that from now on our fate would be in our own hands. We provoked the British, created skirmishes, and stirred up rebellion whenever possible. In one case, we prevented them from entering the camp and threw stones at them. Although the incident was resolved through negotiation and a promise of quiet, it filled us with courage— the courage to embrace freedom.

Friday, 5th of Iyar, 5708, 5.14.1948

It was afternoon when we heard the loud and confident voice of David Ben-Gurion over the loudspeaker: "The State of Israel is established." We were transfixed to the voices of the announcers coming from the loudspeakers. Every item of news drew us that much closer to our freedom and lifted our spirits. The proclamation of the Declaration of Independence met with rising cheers of happiness. Words cannot describe how overwhelmed with joy we were.

The mighty sound of voices singing "Hatikvah"[48] swept through the Cyprus camps. We were a "free nation in our own country." I knew that the day was near when I would be home—in my country, in my state.

The government of the British Mandate had been terminated. The British neither made haste to leave the country, nor to release us. The main reason for our delayed release was their fear that the youngsters among us would enlist and participate in the war that was raging in Israel, the War of Independence. Therefore, the first ships leaving for Israel carried the elderly, women, and children.

I waited impatiently for my turn to arrive.

At the beginning of January 1949, I too was on board. The waves were taking me home. Three years of longing for Israel and for freedom had passed. I was on my way to the only place in the world in which I belonged. My happiness was boundless. My breath stopped when I saw the shore of the Promised Land and the beauty of the Carmel Mountains. My heart was bursting with joy.

The sound of ships' sirens welcomed us at Haifa Port. There were crowds of people cheering our arrival, as though the whole country was embracing us.

I walked down the gangplank filled with emotion, smiling

---

48   Israel's national anthem

from ear to ear. As I stepped on the ground, taking my first step on *Eretz Israel*, two young men from the military police held me on each side and led me to the registration station. The two policemen were speaking Hebrew and I answered them in Yiddish. Once registered, they again accompanied me to a bus that was waiting for young people like me. The bus filled up quickly and after a short ride, it stopped and we disembarked.

Atlit Military Camp.
My first stop at home.

My first few hours included being assigned to a tent containing a *Sochnut*[49] bed and a blanket, organizing my new abode, and making new friends. Night departed, making way for a fresh *Shabbat* morning. At breakfast, I noticed that some of the people with whom I had become acquainted had disappeared.

After investigating and surveying the area, I noticed a hole in the fence through which people were leaving the camp, running to the road, and hitching rides. I later learned that people this was the Haifa-Tel Aviv highway by which people wished to reach the big city. Without thinking twice, I left the camp in the very same way, running toward the road as they did. We ran toward a bus parked at the side of the road. We

---

49 A metal bed frame, named after the *Sochnut*, the Jewish Agency that provided this as part of the standard new immigrant's kit.

door of the bus was open and a military policeman was sitting on the front seat.

"Come in, come in!" he invited me politely and in a friendly manner. I went inside. Once the bus had filled up with passengers and the door shut closed, we were all promptly driven straight back to the camp. Apparently, the camp authorities knew about the gap in the fence and the strong desire of its inhabitants to feel independent in the large city. They knew that people were sneaking out and permitted them to feel victorious, albeit for a short time. However, the country was fighting for its independence and these people were essential to the defense of the country.

After a short preliminary course given in the various languages of the immigrants, we were enlisted. I was enlisted in the transport force of the Israeli army, following my experience as a truck driver in the Russian army. It is difficult to say that we were fully trained as soldiers or that we understood what we were up against. In retrospect, I understand that there was no alternative. The country needed each and every one of us.

On the assigned day, we presented ourselves at the trucks and made our way to Sarafand.[50] Sarafand had previously been a large British military base that had been vacated by the British forces on 5.15.1948, one day after the proclamation of Israel's independence. Soldiers of the Arab Legion had been allowed into the base through the Jerusalem Gate by the British, and started showering Rishon LeZion with fire. After several days, the base was captured by *Givati* soldiers.

---

50   Now known as Tzrifin.

Our truck was now making its way through that same Jerusalem Gate into the army base of Tzrifin. The entrance was magnificent, with its upright eucalyptus trees on both sides. We found evidence of the presence of Arabs in the residences and the canteen.

We were assigned to rooms. My driving and mechanical skills were tested. After a short briefing in Hebrew—translated into Yiddish—we were sent on our way. The command believed that, with time, we would become acclimatized, learn Hebrew, and understand the purpose of our being enlisted in the army.

I was stationed on the southern front as a driver of vans and trucks purchased from the American and British armies. The commentator Y. Ben-Israel wrote: "The achievements of the transport force were of vital importance, especially on the southern front."

I was discharged from army service in 1951, at the Ariel air force camp, located in Yehuda Hayamit Street in Jaffa. I became a free civilian in my own country.

CHAPTER 9:
Home

"A country is not its fields, hills, forests, or guns. It is, above all, its children."

- Janusz Korczak

Two issues confronted me on my release from the army in 1951—lodgings and livelihood. My new friend, Israel Waldinger, came to my assistance by suggesting that I move into one of the washrooms located on the rooftops of the residential buildings that had been fenced off as the Ariel military base. He told me, "I have occupied one of those washrooms. There is another laundry room next to it, on the same roof. I can take you there, if you wish." I indeed wished to check out that option.

Together we made for the roof that was to become my new home. The laundry room proved to be a niche, closed off by a door. The sink and faucet had formerly been used by the housewives residing in the building for doing the laundry.

After a quick look around, I came to the conclusion that there would indeed be room for a bed and I settled into my room. I locked my room from the inside and was eager to go out and start my new life.

The problems of the fence surrounding the camp and the regimental policeman sitting at its entrance were easily solved. First of all, I soon became known as a resident of the place, and secondly, there were many loopholes and secret passages in and out of the camp.

A chance encounter with my old friend Zeev Gurfinkel secured me a place of employment. Zeev had participated in the battle over Jerusalem, at the end of which he found employment with a building contractor who owned a factory that manufactured storerooms and modular structures. I was also employed there and became a building assembler, a job that took me all over the country.

I was once again a driver during my army reserve duty. During Operation Kadesh,[51] I was stationed in the runway unit of the air force. As its name implies, I was in charge of transporting all required equipment for the runways for the airplanes and helicopters.

We reached El Arish and were the first to break into the airport, which the Egyptians had abandoned in their flight. This signaled the closing of a circle for me, since the British had blockaded the illegal immigrants' ship I was on the *Af Al Pi Chen* at El Arish.

---

51   The Sinai Campaign

Painter, sculptor, and artist

At the end of the Sinai Campaign in 1957, after six months of reserve duty, I was finally out of my army uniform. I wasted no time in fulfilling my dream, and registered for art and painting courses at the Avni Institute of Art and Design, then on Ben Yehuda Street in Tel Aviv. The Avni Institute is known for the many artists and designers that passed through its gates as teachers or students, among them Yehezkel Streichman, Moshe Sternschuss, Moshe Mokady, Marcel Janco, Avigdor Stematsky, and others. What a wonderful period this was! My four years of study opened a whole new world to me.

We were a close and intimate group of students. My peers were Avraham Korkin, Itzchak Leblank, Lior Rotem, who later became a television director, Uri Naeh, the architect Yaakov Komlush, and the one and only Malvina Kaplan.

I will always remember Dr. Eugen Kolb, art lecturer and the first director of the Tel Aviv Museum. Dr. Kolb's lectures were thrilling, enriching, and opened up new horizons of magical lands to me. I signed up for another course with Dr. Kolb so I could hear his lectures again, which never failed to enchant me. The lessons were mainly about Abstract art although we also tried out Expressionism, the artistic style based on expressions, impressions, and experiences.

Having completed my courses, I passed the examinations and was awarded an official certificate signed by the Ministry of Education and Culture. This was valuable and significant to me. Since my studies at Avni were evening classes, I continued working at the Tel Aviv Municipality during the mornings, moving to different positions, as I did to various places of residence.

Zeev and I decided to become residents of Tel Aviv, and we rented a room in a temporary hut in the Mahlul neighborhood. Mahlul was a neighborhood of temporary huts established by the government of the British Mandate in the 1920s. Parallel to the sea coast, its borders were the Muslim cemetery to the north (next to the Hilton Hotel) and KKL Boulevard (today Ben-Gurion Boulevard) to the south. At first it served as temporary dwelling places for the immigrants of the Third *Aliyah*[52] and for Jewish refugees from Jaffa escaping the *Tarpa*[53] riots. The name Mahlul was derived from Ottoman law, which defined uncultivated land as violated and undesirable land. According to that same law, any building became legal as soon as it had a roof above it. Thus, Mahlul sprang up with unlicensed structures that were made out of huge containers and wooden beams, obviously not paying any city tax. The neighborhood was called *Shchunat Hap*.[54]

I have been a resident of Tel Aviv ever since.

---

52   The third wave of Zionist immigration to Palestine from Europe between 1919 and 1923.

53   The Me'oraot Tarpa (Jaffa) riots were a series of violent riots in Mandatory Palestine.

54   "Hap" means "grab" in Yiddish.

Shoshi

She was beautiful, pleasant, kind, and she captured my heart. I met her in 1960 during my studies at Avni. Rosa Bohana, known as Shoshi. We fell in love, and at the end of a wonderful year of friendship, decided to get married on the completion of my studies.

The end of my studies was drawing near. My friends and I decided to attend a course in Paris, the dream of any artist. I was once again at a crossroad. On the one hand, my dream of setting up home with my heart's desire; and on the other … I decided to travel to Paris. Shoshi also made her decision—she was breaking up with me. We parted, and it seemed as if there was no going back.

A day passed, then another, and then three days. I was missing something, and then I knew that I would have other chances to fulfill my Paris dream. I wanted Shoshi by my side. I unsuccessfully tried to find her again. After about two weeks, while driving a jeep given to me by the municipality for use in my job, I saw her walking on the corner of Allenby and Ben Yehuda streets, near the Mugrabi cinema. I stopped the jeep with a screech of wheels. It took several minutes for her to agree to get into the jeep, and we have been together ever since then. We married in August 1961.

My Shoshi is still beautiful, pleasant, and kind.

Shoshi speaks:

I was born on 9.28.1927 in Mazagan, Morocco, to Shlomo and Sol Bohana. I was named Rosa. My sisters are Anat, Simi, Terese, and Alice, and my brother is Yehuda. My father worked as an inspector at an egg production plant, checking each and every egg under an electric light, for more than twelve hours a day. He was also a musician and played the violin, oud, guitar, and darbuka in a band that entertained people at weddings, bar mitzvah celebrations, and other Jewish festivities.

My mother worked as a seamstress. Her mother, Aziza, my grandmother, lived with us. She ran the household, raised us, and took care of us. Thanks to her, we lacked nothing and always had food and clothing.

I studied at the Alliance school for eight years. The language of study was French. By tradition, the school management provided us with textbooks, lunches, and a gift of shoes on Jewish holidays.

After graduating from school, I began to work to help in supporting the family. This was the usual custom in those days. When I turned seventeen, my sister and I moved to Casablanca, where there were more opportunities for employment. My first job was in a factory that manufactured bed sheets, run by Mr. Zakhaus, a German Jew. Following that, I worked in Dr. Aharon Cohen's clinic for nursing mothers, where I was treated as a daughter.

I longed to make *aliyah* to Israel from the time I came of age. My sister and I were willing to leave in 1948, but my parents and particularly my grandmother refused vigorously to hear of this idea. I gave up my plans out of respect for them.

And then it happened. The date is still fixed in my memory. On Friday, 8.19.1955, I returned home from Casablanca for a holiday. While visiting a married friend of mine, I noticed the deafening silence from the Arab coffee shops on the way. There were no card games or loud music. I shared my feeling of foreboding with my parents, who tried to explain that the Arabs sometimes liked to sit and talk quietly, and that I need not worry.

As usual we had our Friday evening dinner and the following day, at midday, my mother and I went to visit my sister, the mother of a month-old baby. We noticed a group of hundreds or thousands of Arab men and women approaching us. Alarmed, we turned back and returned home. We quickly locked all the doors and windows and went into a sealed room. My brother later returned from a bicycle ride and described what had transpired outside—a mass rampage of angry Arab rioters.

At about six in the evening they reached our home and poured gasoline on the wooden doors, setting them alight. Fortunately, we were able to extinguish the fire using water from the well in our kitchen. Our good neighbor from the Amiel family took us in to her home, which was spacious and protected with heavy doors. We stayed awake that night, crying.

On our return the following day, we were speechless at the sight of the wreckage. Our doors had been burned, doors and windows shattered, and our belongings looted. At about ten o'clock, three young men appeared, brothers from the Alalouf family, and instructed us: "Each one of you is to pack a bag and get onto the van waiting outside." We were taken to the sports hall of the Jewish community center, where we joined another 150 evacuee families.

Wealthy and compassionate families from the community provided us with food and drink. I brought my father a pot of tea from the Abergil family whom I knew, since he was not feeling well. "Where are you staying?" Mrs. Abergil asked. When I told her, she invited us all to her home. A half hour later, we found ourselves in a large room in her home. We had everything that we needed, and of course were given food and drink.

We decided to return to our home and repair the damage. When a representative of the Joint visited us with registration papers for *aliyah* to Israel, we did not hesitate. The month was August. We waited throughout that September, during the month of the Jewish high holidays, with everything we could take with us packed into large crates. We attended our synagogue for the last time on *Sukkot*, and the day after the holiday, we were already on trucks taking us to the collection point. For the next month, we shared a tent with another two families. When our turn arrived, we were taken to the port of Casablanca.

Approximately 400 men, women, and children boarded the *Mugrab*. We were immediately sent down to the ship's belly, sharing the space with Arabs whom the French had exiled to Indochina.[55] We usually stayed on the deck by day

---

55   Vietnam

to avoid the stifling and overcrowded conditions inside, and to keep away from possible friction with the Arabs. There, on the deck, we could breathe fresh air and then return to the ship's belly at night. Fortunately, the sea was calm, and after several days we anchored at Marseilles in France. We were taken from Marseilles to Camp du Grand Arénas, a camp that the Germans had built during the Second World War.

Our residence permit allowed us to go into the city. The first site we visited was the fish market, where the fishwives regarded us suspiciously. If we dared to say anything derogatory about the quality of the fish, we were met with a barrage of curses. We also visited luxury stores, in which we ascended and descended the escalators, which were a novelty for us. Again, the response of the locals was, "These refugees!"

Our month-long wait at the camp for a month finally came to an end. My sister, her husband, and the baby boarded the luxury liner *Jerusalem*, while we sailed one week later on a more modest ship called *Negbah*. We were excited to encounter the Hebrew-speaking *tzabar*[56] sailors, and sat in a circle singing with a young man who played "Johnny Guitar" on his guitar.

On the evening of Saturday, 11.19.1955, we docked at Haifa Port. We had arrived home. We were delighted by the view of the flickering lights of the Carmel seen from afar. We disembarked the following morning and entered the passenger hall, where we were offered a warm glass of milk. Each family was called up in turn to register behind a screen.

---

56   Israeli

We were sprayed with DDT, not knowing whether to laugh or cry. We brushed this aside, thrilled to be in Israel. We and another two families found ourselves in a van, equipped with two loaves of bread, twelve eggs, and potatoes.

Our destination was *Ma'abara*[57] *Hatzor Alef.* We were provided with a two-room caravan, kitchenette, bathroom, shower, beds, and two blankets. There was no electricity or water. Outside there was a water faucet. We immediately started organizing ourselves. We set up our home with our belongings from our personal suitcases and we felt blessed with what we had.

"Why did you come here?" asked some of the local veterans. "There is no food, no employment, and nowhere to bury the dead. They are placed in cold storage." We blocked our ears and refused to listen to the slander. One of our neighbors from our town in Morocco came to our assistance with cutlery and crockery until our crates arrived with all our belongings. We stayed inside most of the time, leaving the caravan only to acquire supplies, since it was raining during the days of our arrival.

We decided to seek employment two weeks after our arrival. On the bus to Tiberias, we noticed that all of our fellow passengers were carrying black bags. We thought that they were probably clerks on their way to work. We soon realized our mistake. During the trip, the bags opened up and everyone started eating food they had brought for the journey.

We traveled from Tiberias to Kibbutz Afikim. A pleas-

---

57   Transit camp in Israel

ant young French-speaking man from Tunisia translated the words, which meant, "We are not accepting you." We returned to our home impoverished, as the bus fare had left us very little to buy provisions for *Shabbat*. I then determinedly took a bus to Haifa. With the help of an interpreter, I explained to the official that I wished to join an *ulpan*[58] in Jerusalem. "Very well, you may join, on condition that you sign a promissory note that, on finding employment, you pay back the money for five months of study at the ulpan, including food and lodging. The amount is three hundred *lirot* in installments." I signed and left for Jerusalem, sharing a room at the *ulpan* with another two women.

Learning Hebrew was very difficult at first, but I persevered. After five months of study at the *ulpan*, I returned to my parents at Hatzor. One week after my return, I was called up to enlist by a policeman who arrived at the *ma'abara*. "What was your occupation in Morocco?" I explained that I had worked in a clinic for nursing mothers. "My mother-in-law is a department manager in the Ministry of Health in Tiberias. I will submit your papers to her," he said.

I was accepted for employment doing the night shift at a nursing home in Kiryat Shmona as part of the team led by Dr. Salmanovicz and the head nurse Sara Bodek. The nursing home was a hut consisting of several rooms. Although I worked shifts of twelve hours or more, I was paid for only eight hours of work, once every three or four months.

I worked at the nursing home for two years, later moving

---

58   A school for the intensive study of Hebrew.

over to Assaf Harofe Hospital. After seven months of work there, I realized that working in shifts was not for me and decided to become a nursemaid to two children. My employers, the Denishevsky family, adopted me as a daughter in their home at 84 Ben Yehuda Street. Here my wages were good and was paid on time.

At that time, my brother was working in Tel Aviv and making a good living. Together, we managed to purchase an Amidar apartment in Jaffa for ourselves and our parents. The apartment contained two rooms and a large hall.

Surrounded by many friends in Tel Aviv, I became acquainted with a young man who was studying painting and sculpture at the Avni Institute. His name was Itzchak Belfer. I was thirty-four and he was thirty-seven when we met. We spent much time together, watching movies, taking walks, drinking coffee at Kassit, and going to the beach. Our friendship strengthened and we fell in love. Marriage was on the horizon.

One day, walking out of a movie house in Tel Aviv with Itzchak, I felt that something was amiss. "What is wrong?" I asked "I'm thinking of going to Paris with a friend," he answered. I said, "Have a good time!" and we each went our own way.

For three weeks, I forced myself to keep away from the places we used to visit together. I did not want to see him. One day, waiting at the number 7 bus stop to Jaffa, somebody sounded a horn. I recognized the sound and knew it was Itzchak in his jeep, but I did not look his way. He carried on hooting. I turned around and after he implored me to join him, I got into the jeep. I told him that I was going to meet my parents who were coming from Rosh Pina. Itzchak took me home. We made a date to meet that evening, and we have been together ever since.

We were lawfully married in my parents' home in the presence of my family and friends on Wednesday 8.9.1961. Our first home was the hut in Mahlul. My parents did not know that I was living in a hut. When the owner of the hut paid us 500 *lirot* to vacate the premises, we took out a bank loan and went searching for another apartment.

Apartment hunting was difficult in Tel Aviv in those days, especially when we were asked, "Are you white or black?" meaning, are you Sephardic or Ashkenazi? We nevertheless managed to find a small penthouse apartment on Gordon 9, sold to us by Mr. Zersky for key money for the sum of 7,500 lirot with a monthly payment of eighteen lirot. This was to be our home for the next thirty-eight years. Our son, Haim, was born here on 11.19.1962.

Haim

Itzchak: It was difficult to contain the waves of emotion I felt on that day when I became a father. I'm a father! I have a son! We are a family. During the long hours of waiting for the birth to take place, I walked around, wondering whether it would be a girl or a boy. I decided to visit my office at the municipality, hoping that I would calm down among familiar faces and stop worrying about Shoshi. My friends welcomed me at the office.

"The hospital called. Your wife has given birth. *Mazel tov!*"

I first saw my son through the window of the nursery. My child. I was beside myself with delight. After the *brit* ceremony attended by family and friends, we returned home, mother, father, and son, floating on the clouds, touching the miracle that had happened, but not yet able to comprehend it. Haim, we named you after my late father.

Haim speaks: It is Saturday in a small but charming penthouse on Gordon Street in Tel Aviv. It has a huge balcony overlooking the blue sea. This is my parents' home. I am a small boy. My mother wakes me up, gently and patiently, with a wide smile on her face. A hug, an embrace, a kiss, a kind word. I am enveloped in love, ready for a new day. She turns to the kitchen to prepare breakfast and I go out to the balcony toward my father's workroom. Steeped in his art, my father feels my presence and with a warm and wide smile, invites me in to join him.

There is a large painting on the easel, one of the paintings depicting the Holocaust, which my father often commemorates on paper or canvas. Occasionally, the drawings frighten me and I go out to play on the balcony. My father usually explains what the drawings are about, making a place for me at his side, and preparing a small easel for me. He places a clean sheet of paper on it and gives me a charcoal pencil or a brush and paints. Both of us dive into our creative work.

We stop working when my mother calls us to come out to the balcony for breakfast, which always includes *challah* and a bowl filled with black and green olives.

I cling to the above image, ingrained in my memory. It is an accurate reflection of my childhood years in which I received an education based on the doctrine of Janusz Korczak. This meant love, respect for human beings, and mutual respect, sharing, consideration, attentiveness, and most importantly, independence.

Shoshi: I remember when Haim and I went to register for first grade at Tel Nordau School, his small hand in mine. "What does your father do?" the principal asked him. "My father draws the Holocaust," he answered. Stunned, the principal thought that he had not heard correctly and repeated the question. Haim gave the same answer. I nodded to the principal that this was true.

Itzchak: I heard about the conversation through Shoshi. Haim's answer made me wonder whether it was right to expose such a small child to the meaning of my activities. After much thought, I decided that I could not protect my child from the truth, and I have never concealed anything about our lives from him.

I have no doubt that the way I educate my son is influenced by what I absorbed as a child in Dr. Korczak's home. The doctor's doctrine is my guiding principle. Our home is managed according to the spirit of humanity.

Haim: My parents are working people and they have always known how to combine their duties with investing all their efforts in raising me, their child, through education and varied experiences.

The sea was my playground. My father and I would go there on wonderful outings, voyages that included stories that were instructional and educational. These were never forced on me or told in a patronizing manner, as though the adult has all the knowledge; rather, they were told to me while swimming or playing in the sand. We still enjoy the bond of togetherness while walking along the promenade.

There were always boundaries in my education, not based on parental authority, but rather for purposes of explanation and reasoning, even if these were not always to my liking. In the same breath, I will add that although I was an only child, I was never deprived of participation in activities with my peers through pampering or excessive concern.

We have, for many years, and still do, discuss and relate stories from the past, about my father's childhood at the orphanage, about Janusz Korczak and his educational heritage. These conversations accompany me in my life choices, internal conflicts, and decisions.

As an educator and teacher at the Herzliya Hebrew Gymnasium, when asked about the effect of the education I received from home, the answer is obviously that this is my life!

Itzchak: Haim is everything to me in my life—its essence, content, and reason. I cannot, even for a minute, imagine my life without him, without my son, the person who grew up beside me, who has such an effect on my life and that of his mother Shoshi. I see his development as my own. I am totally at ease in his company, with no divisions or barriers.

My son served in the army for twenty-two years and was discharged as a lieutenant-colonel, a naval officer, and engineer in the Israeli navy. One day, he said, "Dad, I do not wish to continue working as an engineer and manager. I want to be a teacher and educator." I was moved with emotion. An educator, in my eyes, is sacred. He is a person who devotes himself to his work, irrespective of the pay he receives. Education is one of the most important professions and I am proud that my son chose it.

The most valuable gift Haim has given us is our two granddaughters: Neta, at present a soldier, and baby Alma, from his marriage to Efrat, whom we love as a daughter. We have been blessed and we look to the future with hope.

The monument at Gunzburg, Germany. A general view

CHAPTER 10:

An Unfinished End

"The world can become a better place through education alone."

- Janusz Korczak

Parallel to my employment in the public works department of Tel Aviv Municipality, I was asked to be responsible for the art collection of the municipality and its institutions. At that time, I set up drawing classes for municipality employees, with the cooperation of the workers' union. Several courses were opened and I was to fulfill my dream of sharing my knowledge and contributing to others. We held the courses in the building of the Workers' Organization on Pompadita Street.

After my early retirement at the age of sixty, I continued teaching for many years at the *Universita Amamit*[59] in Tel Aviv, to my great enjoyment. I am proud that among my students were my wife and son. There is no doubt that my retirement years have done me good. I have become the master of my own time and am free to draw, read, do research, and enrich my world. I have the feeling of liberation, as a person who has been given the opportunity of a lifetime.

As a member of the Janusz Korczak Association, I have held numerous meetings and lectures with pupils and teachers in which I spoke about the doctor, about his educational methods, and life in his midst at the orphanage. I hold these meetings on a voluntary basis and regard it as my privilege and blessing to pass the legacy of Dr. Janusz Korczak on to the younger generation, for many of whom this is their first encounter with Dr. Korczak's image, character, work, and writings.

In addition, I have held and am still holding exhibitions on the topics of:

1. Dr. Korczak and the orphanage
2. The Holocaust

Main Exhibitions:

1967 Individual exhibition—Eretz Israel Museum, Ramat Aviv, Ethnography and Folklore Wing

1968 Individual exhibition—Yad Lebanim Museum, Rehovot

1969 Individual exhibition—Ghetto Fighters' House Museum

1970 Individual exhibition—Ramat Gan Museum

1971 Individual exhibition—Yad Vashem Museum

1972 Individual exhibition—Tzavta Cultural Center

1973 Individual exhibition—Judah L. Magnes Museum

1975 Individual exhibition—Paris (UNESCO) International convention on Janusz Korczak

1977 Individual exhibition—Massuah Museum, Tel Yitzchak. Awarded The Nahum Gutman Prize on the Subject of the Holocaust

1981 Group exhibition—Binyenei Ha'uma, Jerusalem,

1984 Individual exhibition—Haifa Theater

1988 Joint exhibition with Aba Foyvel, "Pictures From Detention Camps and the Ghetto"

1992   Individual exhibition—Yad Vashem Museum, Jerusalem, marking fifty years since Janusz Korczak was murdered

1994   Individual exhibition—Wohlin House, Yad Vashem, Center for Holocaust Education, Givatayim

1998   Wuppertal University—Gottingen School

1998   Art Academy of Berlin, Germany

2000   Bernard Gallery, Tel Aviv

2003   Individual exhibition— "The Return of Janusz Korczak to Ein Harod"—Beit Haim Sturman, Ein Harod Ihud

2003   Unveiling of Monument in Memory of Janusz Korczak and his Children, Gunzburg, Germany

2005   Individual exhibition—National Conference for Teachers, Płock, Poland

2006   Individual exhibition—Beit Yad Lebanim, Rishon LeZion

2007   Individual exhibition as part of the exhibition in memory of Janusz Korczak and his work—the Jewish Museum, London, England

2010   Individual exhibition as part of the exhibition in memory of Janusz Korczak and his work—Holocaust Museum, Johannesburg, South Africa

* Many other exhibitions have been held in schools and cultural centers all over Israel.

I have also been blessed with a son who understands the importance of my work and the weight I give my lectures about Janusz Korczak in schools and other educational frameworks, since these are the things that I feel I have to do. Ever since my son became a civilian, his integration into my worlds of art and my educational work have afforded me great satisfaction.

I vividly remember the exhibition he organized for me on the *Af Al Pi Chen*, in cooperation with the director of the museum. On the opening evening, the head of the Israeli navy honored me with his presence. The exhibition was held on the very ship that carried me deep inside its belly as a refugee to safety. It closed a circle for me, since the exhibition displayed art that I had created from the depths of my soul and impressions of my past, which I had created as a free person in my own country.

For many years, I refused to step on the land of Germany and, in particular, to display my work there. One day, the telephone rang. The caller was Professor Friedhelm Beiner, a lecturer at Wuppertal University, who told me about a course on the topic of the Holocaust, which was opening there. "I have heard about your work from a mutual friend, Leon Harari," he said, requesting me to hold a lecture and an exhibition for students at the university. I declined, owing to my feelings and attitude toward Germany. I added, "I believe that you are the first person to whom I have ever spoken German since the Holocaust." That was the end of the conversation. I put the phone down. However, the man did not give up.

We met again at a meeting held by the Janusz Korczak Association at Kibbutz Lohamei Hageta'ot. Professor Dauzenroth stood next to Professor Beiner, and they both tried to persuade me to dismiss my objection to visiting Germany. They reasoned: "It is for the younger generation of Germany. This is a generation that knows nothing and, to our regret, is not being taught about the Holocaust. These students need to know what happened." My refusal held firm.

Determined, Professor Beiner arrived in Israel to interview the children of Janusz Korczak's orphanage. He told us that he and Professor Dauzenroth were about to translate the sixteen volumes of Janusz Korczak's writings from Polish into German. "Please come to Germany with your exhibition when the books are published," they asked.

I conferred with my family and with other former children of the orphanage. Their opinion was unanimous. The aim of disseminating awareness of the Holocaust, especially among German students and youth, obliged me to travel to Germany. After several months, when Professor Beiner called to tell me that the exhibition hall was ready, I gave him a positive answer.

I flew to Germany with Shoshi, my moral support, my source of encouragement and strength. On landing in Germany, the sound of the German language overwhelmed me with memories, sights, and the oppressive and heavy load I have borne my whole life. We were warmly and respectfully received by Professor Beiner and the other hosts. I placed my exhibition inside the Synagogue of Wuppertal, which was inactive at that time. The space had been especially prepared for that purpose.

I delivered a lecture to a packed hall on the opening night. The encounter with the students was difficult since I preferred to speak in Polish, with an interpreter translating my words. I felt that my German was not good enough to be able to convey the intensity of my emotions. The youngsters were spellbound.

At the end of the lecture, it was time for questions. One of the students asked: "According to your lecture, Mr. Belfer, there seems to be a contradiction between what you have told us and the appearance of your works of art in the exhibition. You told us that you were not in the forced labor or concentration camps, but your art depicts those camps and the people in them. How do you explain that?"

My answer was short. "You are correct. I was not there physically, but when I escaped from the ghetto, I left my mother, grandparents, three brothers, and two sisters there. I was with them in spirit. I do not know where they were murdered, in the ghetto, or in the death camps. However, I was there too." There was dead silence in the hall.

Since then, I have held numerous lectures and exhibitions in Germany on the topics of Dr. Korczak's doctrine and the Holocaust. My most prominent work there was the monument I created in memory of Janusz Korczak and the children on their last path outside a girls' school in Gunzburg. Mr. Siegfried Steiner, the chairman of the Janusz Korczak Association of Germany, together with his wife Brigitte, promoted the construction of the monument and it is thanks to them that this project took shape.

A special story accompanies the construction of the monument. The family of the notorious Dr. Mengele lives in Gunzburg and they were obviously opposed to the monument.

However, their opposition was suppressed by the democratic majority, the younger generation, and the Mayor of Gunzburg. The monument is a landmark in the city of Gunzburg to this day.

www.itzchakbelfer.com
www.itzchakbelfer.com

CPSIA information can be obtained
at www.ICGtesting.com
Printed in the USA
FSHW021927010120
65646FS

9 781981 480067